BEGINNER'S GUIDE TO

ADOBE® PHOTOSHOP® ELEMENTS®

MICHELLE PERKINS

AMHERST MEDIA, INC. ■ BUFFALO, NY

ACKNOWLEDGMENTS

Thank you to photographers Barbara Rice and Jeff Smith for generously granting me permission to use their images in several places throughout this book. To see more of their work, check out their books from Amherst Media (www.amherstmedia.com).

Thanks also to: Margaret Beiter, Mary Beiter, Jamie Rae Conley, Chloe and Natalie Karmazyn, Jon Grant, Madeleine Lynch-Johnt, Kathryn Neaverth, Liam Neaverth, Declan O'Leary, Brian Perkins, Cody Perkins, Tom Tran, and Jessica Wright.

Additional thanks to Barbara Lynch-Johnt and Paul Grant for tireless proofreading and many helpful suggestions.

Finally, this is for my Dad, whose interest in photography while I was growing up had a bigger impact on me than he probably knows.

Published by:
Amherst Media, Inc.
P.O. Box 586
Buffalo, N.Y. 14226
Fax: 716-874-4508
www.AmherstMedia.com

Publisher: Craig Alesse
Assistant Editor: Barbara A. Lynch-Johnt

ISBN: 1-58428-138-3
Library of Congress Card Catalog Number: 2003112494

Printed in Korea.
10 9 8 7 6 5 4 3 2 1

[redacted]

Table of Contents

CHAPTER ONE

Getting Started

In this chapter, you'll learn the basic concepts of digital imaging—the terms and ideas you need to get started. These are things you'll need to know as you work on every image, so take the time to read each section thoroughly.

INTRODUCTION

Whether you just like to snap photos of your kids or aspire to be the next Ansel Adams, Elements has the tools you need to perfect your images.

Let's admit it. We've all taken pictures and thought, "If only . . ."—if only Mom's eyes weren't closed, if only there wasn't that ugly light switch on the wall, if only the exposure wasn't so dark. The list goes on and on.

Believe it or not, this isn't a problem that's unique to amateur photographers. Professionals face the same problems with badly timed blinks, less-than-desirable backgrounds, problem exposures, etc. So how do they end up with photos that look so good? Well, a lot of it is knowing how to avoid those pesky problems in the first place (that's what makes them pros!), but another key element is the ability to fix problems after the fact.

For most professional photographers, the software used to accomplish these post-shoot corrections is Adobe Photoshop. While this is, indeed, a powerful imaging tool, most nonprofessionals find it either intimidating, too complex, or just plain too expensive. That's where Elements comes in.

Featuring a user-friendly interface that includes the most commonly used features of Photoshop (as well as a few additional special features) and priced within the budgets of most photo enthusiasts, Elements is all the imaging software most photographers will ever need. With it, you'll be able to correct most of the problems that people experience with their images, do basic retouching (to remove blemishes, soften wrinkles, or even take off ten pounds), and add creative effects that help you make the most of your photos.

What You Need

To use this book effectively, you should have basic computer skills. You don't, however, need to have any specific knowledge of digital imaging or digital imaging software.

Installing Elements

Since clear, step-by-step information on installing Elements is provided with the software itself, you are advised to follow

TIPS AND TRICKS

If this had been an actual "tips and tricks" box, you would be reading some interesting information that would help you make the most of your Elements experience.

Throughout this book, you'll see boxes like these. Don't forget to read them!

those instructions carefully (noting the system requirements listed on the software) and install Elements on your computer before beginning the lessons in this book.

Version and Platform

This book was written using Adobe Photoshop Elements 2.0 on the Macintosh operating system. If you use the software on a Windows system, you will see some very minor variations between the screen shots in the book and what you see on your screen—nothing too tricky, though!

About This Book

This book is organized in quick, two-page lessons. These are designed to take you from the basic concepts (like opening an image), to more complicated digital imaging challenges. Each lesson builds on the skills learned in the previous pages, so you will avoid frustration by ensuring you've really mastered each skill before deciding to move on. Also, don't hesitate to flip back to a previous section if you need to refresh your memory. Elements is a complicated program, and you probably won't absorb everything the first time you read it.

What Images to Use

To try out the techniques, you will also need some digital images to use as "test subjects." You will be best off using a photographic image. You can use your own digital photos, images from a clip-art collection, or film images you have scanned.

You can also download images from this book at no cost from the publisher's web site. To access these images, simply go to www.AmherstMedia.com/downloads.htm, click the link for this book, and enter the password Perk1790. Be sure to read the enclosed PDF file, as it contains important information for using the images. (You'll need Adobe Acrobat to open this PDF file. If it's not already on your computer you can download it for free from www.adobe.com.)

With Elements, it only takes a few seconds to add interesting artistic effects to your digital images.

ALL ABOUT RESOLUTION

Resolution is one of the concepts that people who are new to digital imaging usually find the most confusing. Fortunately, it's not as tricky as it might initially seem to be.

Digital images are made up of dots called pixels. The resolution of an image tells us how close together those dots are (the dots per inch—referred to as the "dpi" of an image). Images with dots that are close together are said to have a "high" resolution (a high number of dots per inch). Images with dots that are far apart are said to have a "low" resolution.

The resolution of an image, to a great degree, determines the apparent quality of the image. High-resolution images tend to look clear and sharp—more like photographs. Low resolution images tend to look grainy, speckled, and blurry. Does this mean you should always create the highest resolution image you can? Well, no. The more dots in an image, the more the computer has to remember and move around every time you ask it to do something with those dots. This means it will take longer for the image to open, and performing operations on it will be slower. Because it is bigger, you'll also need lots of space on your hard drive to store a high-resolution image.

WHICH IS BIGGER?

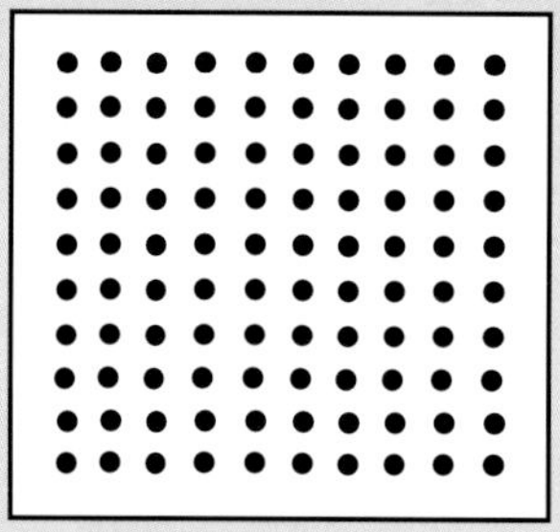

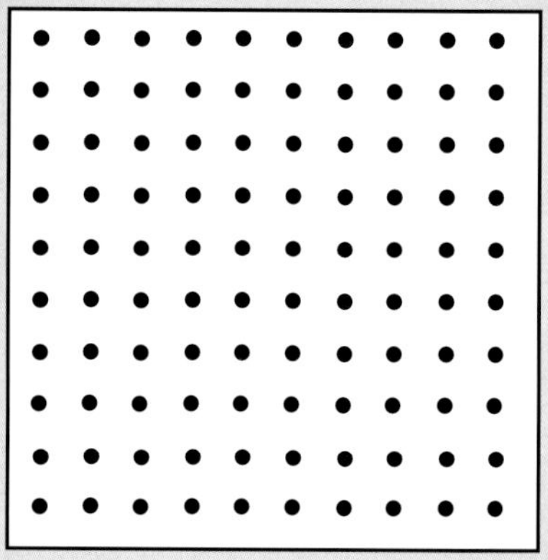

Which is bigger, the image on the left or the one on the right? Actually, it all depends on how you look at it. The image on the right definitely covers more space, but both images are made up of the same number of identical dots. In the image on the left, the dots are tightly packed, giving it a high resolution (a high number of dots per inch). In the image on the right, the dots are far apart, giving it a low resolution (low number of dots per inch). In the digital world, how much "space" an image covers makes very little difference. What counts is how many dots (pixels) it is made of. How many pixels your image should have is determined by what you want to do with it.

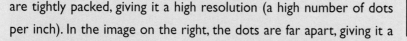

The resolution your image needs to be depends on how you want to use it. The image on the left is at 300dpi, perfect for printing in a book. The image on the right is at 72dpi. This would look just fine on a web site, but its resolution is too low to look good in print.

Which Resolution is Right?

So what should the resolution be? The answer is: only as high as it has to be. The precise number will be determined by what you want to do with the image.

If you want to use it on your web page, you'll select a relatively low resolution—probably 72dpi. This is all that is needed to create an acceptably sharp, clear image on a monitor. Anything more wouldn't make the image look any better and would increase the time the image takes to load.

If you want to generate a photo-quality print on your inkjet printer, you may want to create a file as large as 700dpi. Check the manual that came with your printer for the resolution it recommends for various print settings.

If you'll be having someone else (like a photo lab) print your image, ask them what they recommend.

Changing Resolution

Elements will allow you to change the resolution of an image. As nice as this sounds, though, this doesn't take the place of proper planning.

Elements is great at moving around existing dots (making them closer together or farther apart), and is even pretty skilled at removing dots (reducing resolution). What it doesn't do well is allow you to turn 50 dots into 500 dots. If you ask it to do this, the program will have to guess where to put these dots and what they should look like. Invariably, it won't guess 100 percent successfully, and your resulting image will appear blurry.

In a pinch, you might be able to get away with increasing the resolution by 25 percent—but any more than this and you'll probably not like the results.

Don't Just Guess

If you're not sure what resolution you need to create the product you have in mind, find out before you create your file. There's no point in wasting your time to make complicated refinements on an image that turns out to be unusable. If you'll be using your image in multiple applications (say you want to make a print, but also plan to e-mail the photo to someone), create your image at the largest size you'll need. Make any needed corrections to this large file, then reduce its size and save multiple copies of the image for other uses.

DIGITAL COLOR MODES

When we shoot images on film, we tend to take color for granted and leave it up to the folks at the lab. With digital, we have to know a little bit more to really make our images shine.

If you ever took an art class (or even played around with watercolors as a kid), you probably know that combining two or more colors creates new colors. For example, combining blue paint and yellow paint makes green paint. In fact, almost all colors are actually combinations of some other colors. The exceptions (the colors you can't create by combining others) are called primary colors. In digital imaging, the set of primary colors that are used to create all the other colors in your image is called the color mode.

RGB Mode

If your image is in the RGB mode (the most commonly used mode in Elements), then all of the colors in that image are made up of some combination of red (R), green (G), and blue (B). It may be hard to believe, but by combining just those three colors in slightly different amounts, you can create millions of colors (see page 52). As a result, this is the best mode for working with color images that you really want to look their best. This is the mode that is normally used for on-screen image viewing (like on the Internet) and most photographic printing (like on an inkjet printer or at a photo lab).

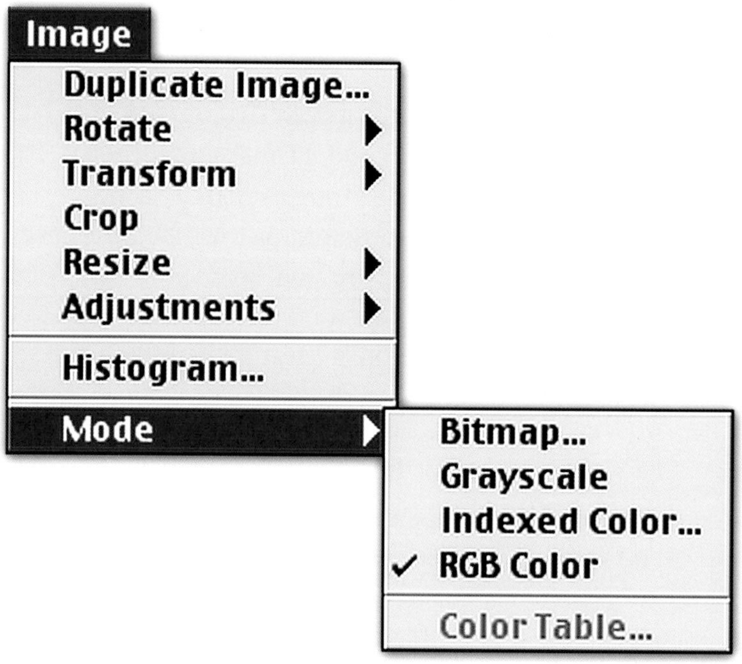

To switch between color modes, just go to Image>Mode and select the desired mode from the pull-down menu.

Grayscale Mode

Another common color mode used in Elements is Grayscale. As you might imagine from the name, all of the colors (well, *tones*, to be more accurate) in this mode are actually shades of gray—exactly like a black & white photograph. In fact, to quickly convert a color image to a black & white one, you can just switch your image to the Grayscale mode by going to Image>Mode>Grayscale.

Indexed Color Mode

This color mode is used for images to be viewed on-screen. It is most useful in situations where perfect image quality is of secondary concern when compared to load time (how long it takes the image to appear on-screen). By limiting the total number of colors in the image to a few hundred (as compared with the millions of colors in RGB), you can get a pretty good-looking image that won't keep viewers of your web site waiting around for your images to load.

Bitmap Mode

This mode uses only black and white pixels (no grays). It's more useful for line art than photos, but it can create some interesting effects. To convert to the Bitmap mode, however, your image must first be in the Grayscale mode.

A Note on CMYK

The CMYK mode is used for professional printing, but it is not supported by Elements. If you need a CMYK image (say, to appear in a book or magazine), you'll need to use Adobe Photoshop to convert it.

To instantly convert a color image to a black & white one, go to Image>Mode>Grayscale to change to the Grayscale mode.

IMAGE FILE FORMATS

They may not seem like much, but those three little letters after the dot in the file name actually tell you a lot about an image. Better yet, they tell other programs how to work with the data in your file.

Think of the file format as the language in which the digital image is written. It tells applications, like word processing software or web browsers, that your file is a picture (rather than a text file, for example) and how it should handle all the data in the file to display it correctly on the screen. The file format is indicated by a tag (.tif, .JPEG, etc.) added after the file name.

Compatibility

If you travel to France and try to speak Portuguese to the natives, you'll likely encounter some comprehension problems. The same thing can happen with some software applications when you ask them to understand a digital file that doesn't speak their language. Elements is exceptionally multilingual; it "speaks" a wide variety of file formats. Other programs aren't as well educated—many recognize only one or two file formats. If you plan to use your digital image in a program other than Elements, read the software's manual to determine what formats it accepts, then save your image accordingly.

Compression

Some file formats give you the option of reducing the amount of memory your computer will need to store an image. This is called compression.

By reducing the amount of memory required to store an image (i.e., the file size), compression allows more images to be stored in a smaller space and permits them to be transmitted over the Internet more quickly. If this sounds too good to be true, don't worry—it is (mostly). Imagine you crush a soda can. It will take up less space, but it will never look like it did to begin with. With digital compression, the same principle applies—of course, it's rather more sophisticated, and your images won't look as bad as your soda can.

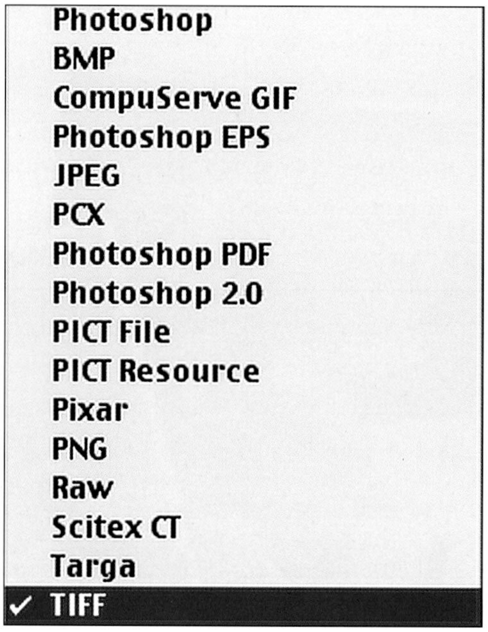

Elements is able to read and write a wide variety of file formats.

When an image is enlarged, you can really start to see the difference in quality between JPEG compression (left) and LZW (right).

When an image is compressed, equations are applied to arrange the data more efficiently or to remove data that is deemed by the software to be extraneous. As a result, your image won't look as good. However, the loss in quality may not be objectionable—or it may be worth it to have an image that loads quickly on your web page.

Two file formats that offer compression are JPEG and TIFF. JPEG offers "lossy" compression, meaning that it removes data and significantly degrades the image. Fortunately, a slider in the JPEG Options window lets you control the degree of compression, so you can compress the file just a little (for better image quality) or a whole lot (when quality isn't as important).

The characteristic grid pattern created by JPEG compression (see above) becomes especially apparent when an image is saved and resaved, compressing it each time. For works in progress, this is not a good file format, but it's standard on the Internet because of the small file sizes it produces.

TIFF offers "lossless" compression called LZW, which doesn't throw anything out (so the image quality remains better), but it also can't compress the image as much.

You can also select ZIP compression from the TIFF Options window. This is similar to LZW, but it adds a layer of protection that helps reduce the likelihood of corruption when files are sent across the Internet. It's a common compression format for Windows users, but Mac users can also open these files if they have StuffIt installed.

In the TIFF Options window (right), you can select no compression, LZW, ZIP, or JPEG compression. In the JPEG Options window (far right), you use the slider at the top of the box to strike the desired balance between file size and image quality. As the file size decreases, so does the image quality.

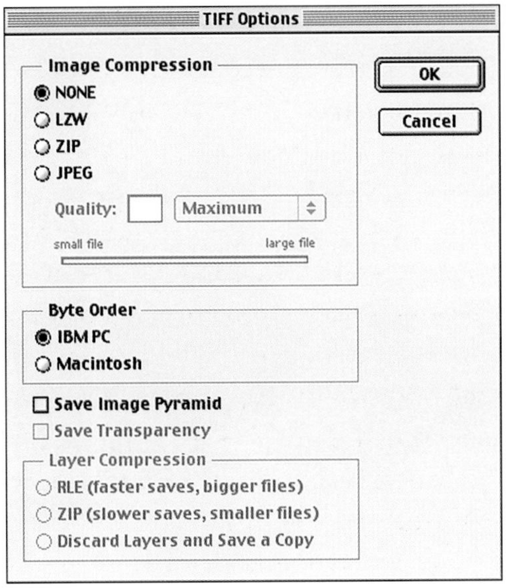

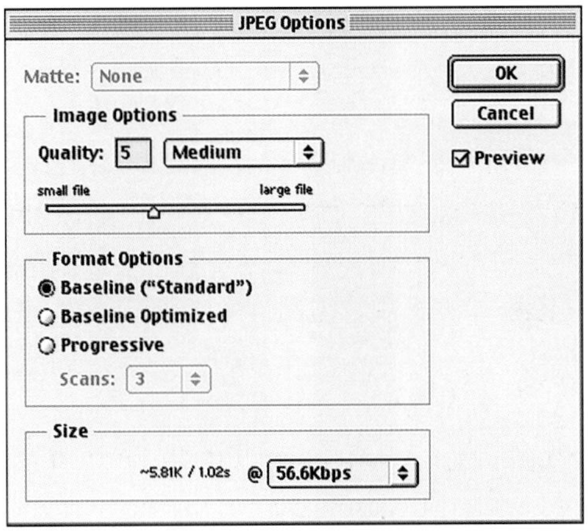

CHAPTER TWO

The Basics

Before you get started making alterations to your images, there are a few more things to learn—like how to view images on-screen for the best results and how to undo any mistakes you might make.

THE WORK AREA

The following is a brief tour that will familiarize you with the landscape of the software. We'll be coming back to all of these features over the course of this book.

The work area in Elements might initially seem a little bit cluttered and overwhelming—there are a *lot* of menus and boxes! However, the workspace tends to combine similar items into related groupings. This makes navigating it much easier.

Menu Bar

The Menu bar runs across the very top of the screen and contains a number of pull-down menus. The following is a brief overview:

File—Open, close, and import files; quit Elements, and more.

Edit—Undo, copy/paste, set preferences for Elements, and more.

Image—Rotate, resize, crop, and make other image adjustments.

Enhance—Adjust the lighting, color, contrast, and more.

Layer—Create, eliminate, or refine layers.

Select—Create, eliminate, or refine selections.

Filter—Select and apply special effects to your image, including artistic looks, sharpening, distortions, and more.

Window—Open and close the various palettes (see page 16–17).

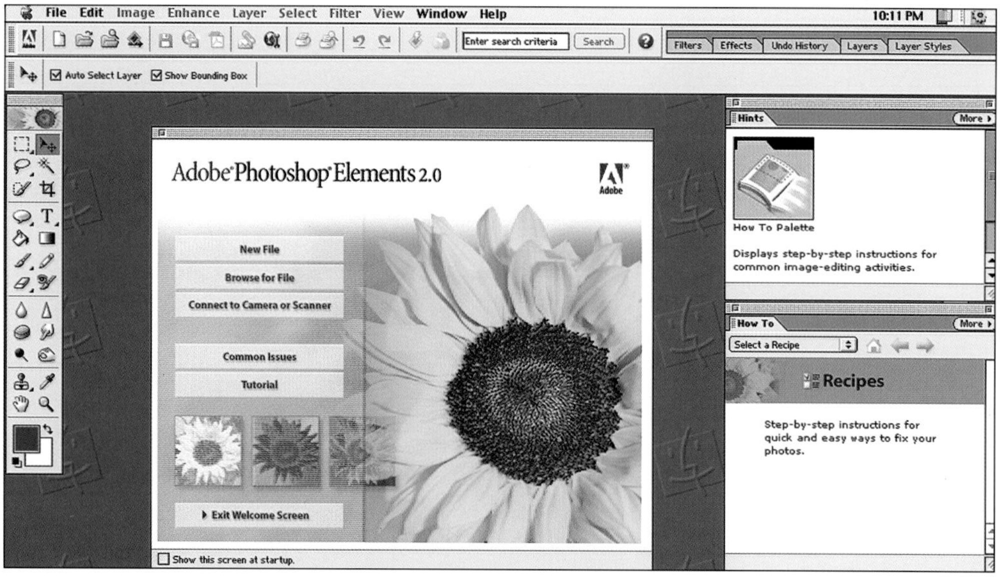

The Elements work area has many palettes, menus, and windows to work with.

Elements Tool Bar

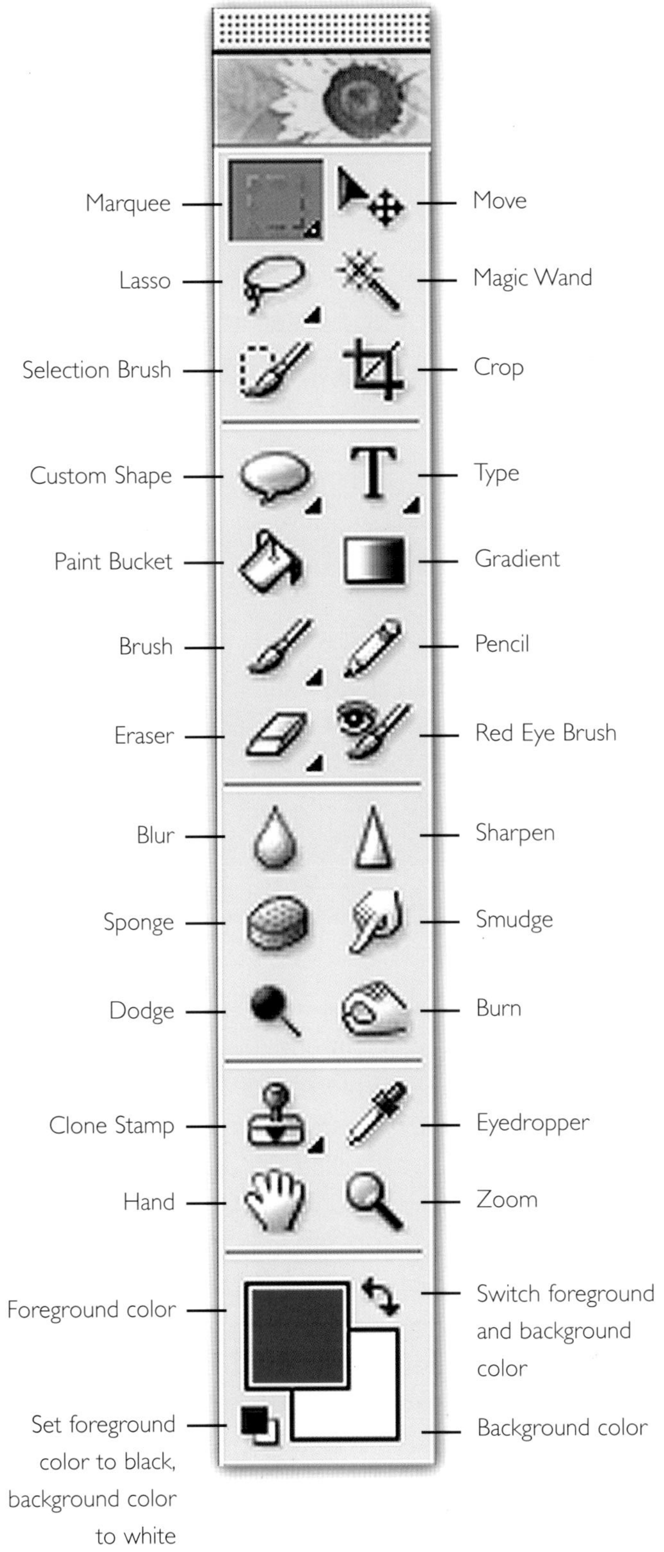

Help—Access to the various help features to rescue you when you're totally stuck (see chapter 3).

Shortcuts Bar

Directly under the Menu bar is the Shortcuts bar. On it are one-click icons for opening and saving files, printing, and more. There's also a search feature—just type in the term you want to look up, hit Search, and Elements will look for it in its help files.

Palette Well

At the far right side of the screen is the Palette Well. For more on this, see pages 16–17.

Options Bar

Beneath the Shortcuts bar is the Options bar. This bar changes depending on which tool is selected, allowing you to customize the function of that tool to your liking.

Palettes

By default, the free-floating Hints and How To palettes are open on the right side of the screen. To customize the available palettes and their location, see pages 16–17.

Tool Bar

At the far left of the screen is the Tool bar. This contains all of the tools you'll need to refine your images—like the Crop tool, Brush tool, Clone Stamp tool, Marquee tool, and more. These will be covered in greater detail later in the book, but to the left is an overview that you may wish to refer back to as you work through the lessons.

WELCOME SCREEN

When you first open up Elements, you'll be greeted by the Welcome screen. From here, you can choose several options for opening images, importing images, or creating new images.

The Welcome screen is a nice resource for getting started. Unless you uncheck the "show this screen at startup" box at the bottom of the window, it will appear every time you open Elements. Once you've clicked on any of the option buttons, the Welcome screen will disappear, but you can get it back by going to Window>Welcome.

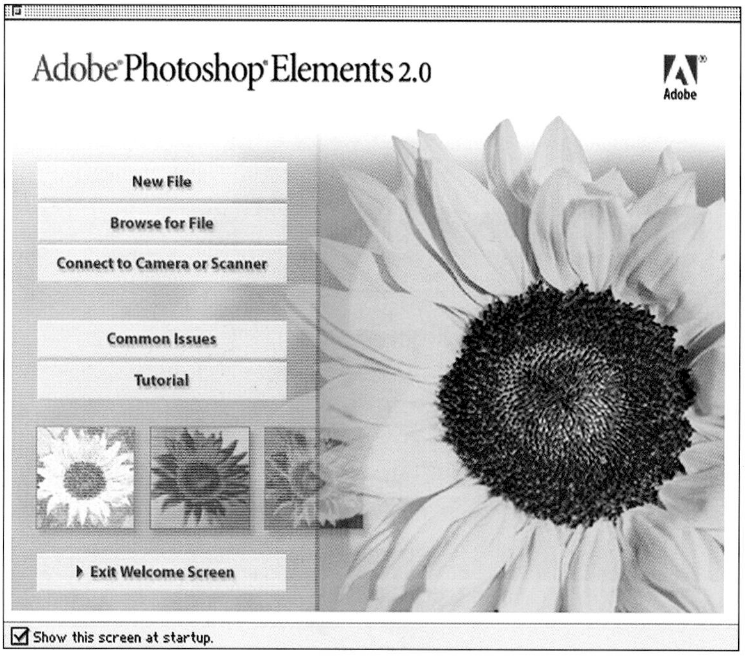

The Welcome screen appears every time you open Elements, giving you quick access to your images.

New File

The top button on the Welcome screen is New File. Clicking on this gives you the digital equivalent of a blank canvas. On this canvas, you can paint or draw, paste items from other sources (in order to make a collage), etc. When you hit New File, the box shown below will appear. In it, you can enter the name of your file, the size you want it to be, the resolution you want (see pages 6–7 for more on this), the color mode (see pages 8–9 for additional information), and what you'd like the color of the canvas to be (for this field, called "contents," white is usually a good choice).

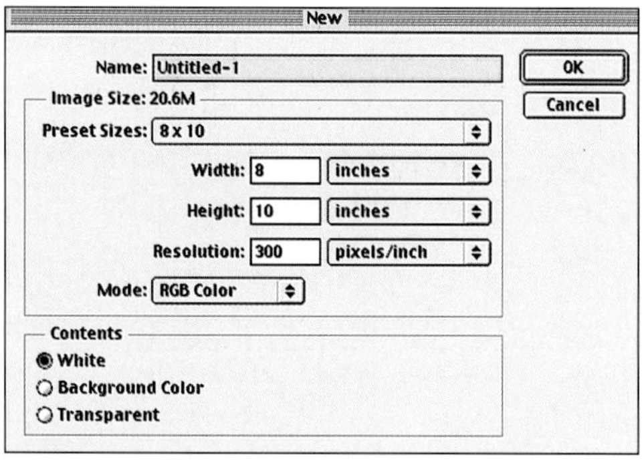

In the New window, you can create a new image, entering exactly the size and resolution you want.

Browse for File

When you hit the Browse for File button, the Browse window will appear. In the top left frame of this window, you select the location where you want to look for your image file. All image files in that area will then be displayed as thumbnails (small images) in the frame

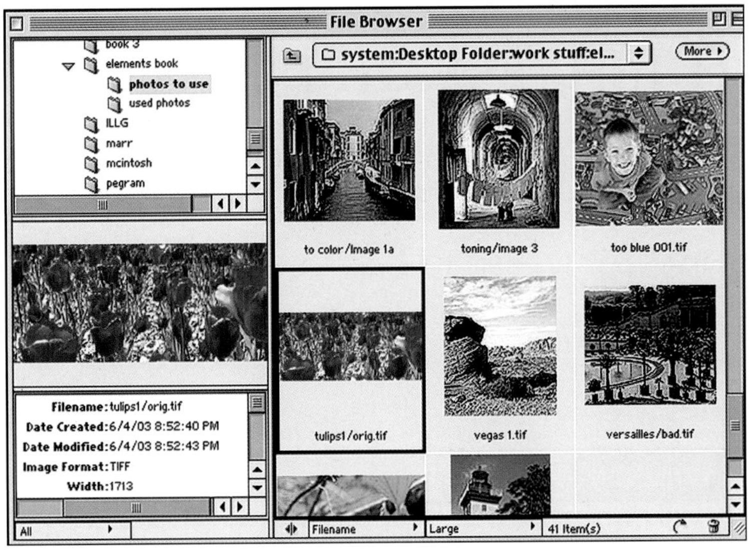

In the File Browser window, you can flip through all the images on your computer (or the media in your computer's various drives) to find the image you want.

on the right. To view a slightly larger version of the image, click on the thumbnail and the image will appear in the middle left frame, with some information about its size, date created, etc., shown in the frame directly below it. Once you've found the image you want to open, double click on it.

Connect to Camera or Scanner

If you have image-acquisition software for a scanner or digital camera installed on your computer, you can access it by hitting the Connect to Camera or Scanner button on the Welcome screen. Then, simply select your scanner software or digital camera image-acquisition software from the pull-down menu in the small window that appears.

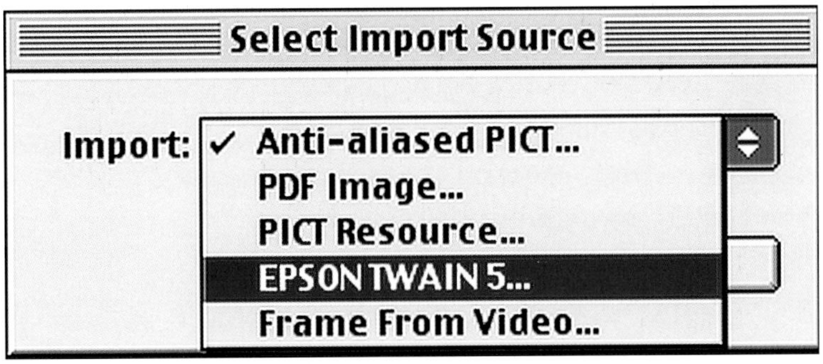

Clicking on Connect to Camera or Scanner activates the Select Import Source window. Choose your scanner or digital camera image acquisition software from the pull down menu and it will open automatically.

File>Open Recent

Often, you won't be able to finish all the work you want to do on an image in one sitting—or you'll have a flash of inspiration about an image you were just working on. For such situations, Elements remembers a short list of the images you have worked on most recently.

To access this list, go to File>Open Recent. Under Open Recent, a submenu will drop down, listing the file names of the images you have recently opened in Elements.

Simply select the correct file from this list and go to work.

ANOTHER OPTION

As you use Elements more and more, you'll probably find that you prefer not to use the Welcome screen—especially if it takes a couple of seconds to load up every time you open the software. To bypass it, unclick the "show this screen at startup" box. You can then create new files by going to File>New, browse for files by going to File>Browse, and connect to your camera or scanner by going to File>Import. Using these commands will open exactly the same windows as hitting the corresponding button on the Welcome screen.

WORKING WITH PALETTES

Elements may well have more palettes to manage than any other program you're accustomed to using—and their presence can be both a blessing and a curse.

Palettes are small windows that help you enhance your pictures by giving you information about your image or offering you options for modifying it. Elements offers eleven palettes that can be viewed in a number of different ways depending on your personal preference. It would be great to be able to have them all visible at once, but unless you work on a system with multiple monitors, this won't leave you much room to view your image.

The following information will make you familiar with the names and functions of the palettes, and the options you have for organizing them.

As you work with Elements, you'll probably find that there are some you use all the time and want displayed prominently. There will be others that you use so rarely that you can just call them up when you need them and then promptly put them away.

The Palettes

The individual palettes and their uses will be covered in detail later in the book as we encounter a need for each. For the meantime, however, a quick way to access any of the palettes is to go to the Window pull-down menu and select the palette you want to open from

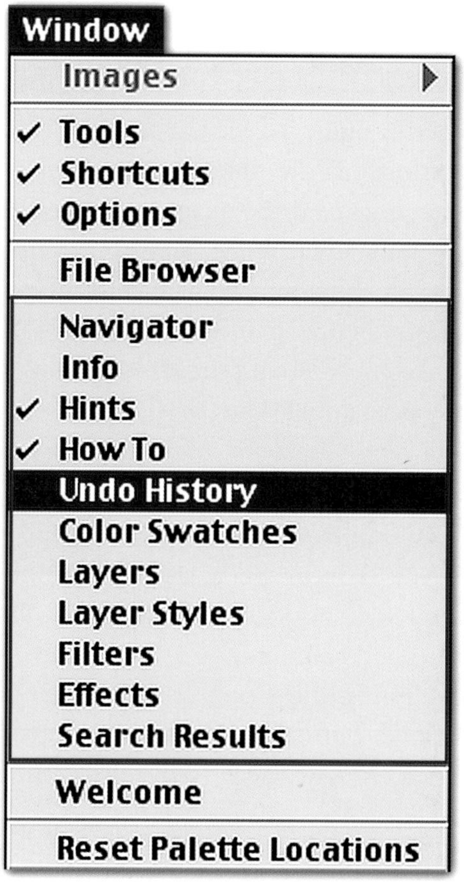

You can open any palette by selecting it from the Window pull-down menu. You can also see which palettes are currently open by noting which ones have check marks.

the list (boxed above in red). This will make the palette appear on your screen. You can also see which palettes are currently open by noting which items in the Window menu are checked.

The Palette Well

The Palette Well is located at the upper-right corner of the screen. It looks like a

The Palette Well contains tabs for various palettes.

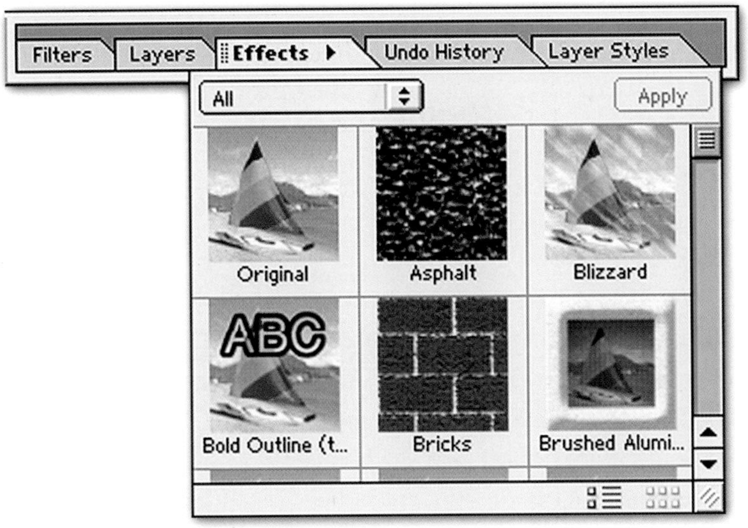

When you click on one of the tabs in the Palette Well, the corresponding palette drops down and is available for use.

series of file folder tabs, each labeled with the name of a palette. To open a palette, just click on the appropriate file tab and the palette will drop down from it. The palette will automatically snap closed as soon as you click anywhere else on your screen.

Out of the Well

To move a palette out of the Palette Well, simply drag the tab out of the well. This will place the palette in a separate, free-floating window that will remain open on your desktop until you put it away.

When you drag palette tabs out of the Palette Well, they appear in free-floating palette windows. You can drag more than one palette into each window to group the palettes as you like. Here, the Layers and Layers Styles menus are in one window.

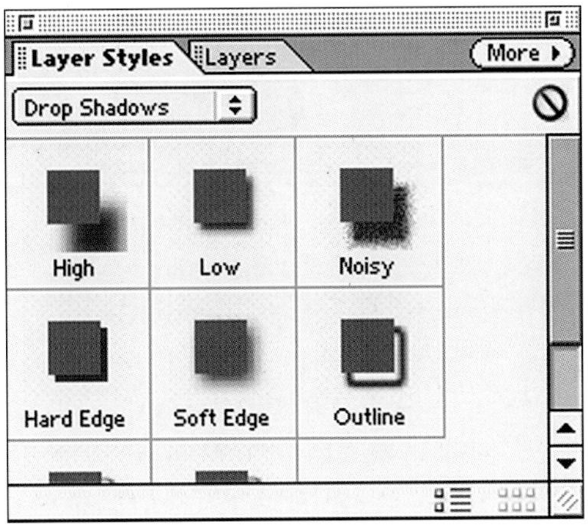

Once you have created one free-floating palette in this way, you can drag other tabs into the same window to create a palette group. The names of the palettes in the group will appear at the top of the window as file tabs. As with the Palette Well, you can access the individual palettes by simply clicking on a file tab.

To return a palette to the Palette Well, simply drag its tab out of the free-floating window and back into the Palette Well.

Minimizing Palettes

When a palette is in a free-floating window, you can minimize the window by double clicking on the palette's file tab. This helps save some space on your computer's screen so you can view your image without as much clutter.

To reduce the size of a palette in a free-floating window, double click on the file tab.

Palette Options

Many palettes have a drop-down menu, labeled More, at their upper-right corner. From this menu you can select additional options for the function of the palette and create custom settings. Since they vary from palette to palette, these options will be discussed later, as we look at the functions of the individual palettes.

VIEWING IMAGES

If you really want to be able to create professional-quality results, you need to learn to view your images well—getting very close so you can refine the tiniest details of the photograph.

A lot of the time, you'll be making corrections or changes to your image as a whole—like adjusting the overall color balance in the photo. In these cases, you'll want to see the whole thing from top to bottom and side to side to ensure your changes aren't having any negative effects on some part of the image you can't see.

There will be other times, however, when you'll want to change just a small part of the image—you might want to remove a small blemish on someone's face, for example. In cases like this, it will help you to be able to enlarge just that portion of the image on the screen so that you can see every detail clearly and work as precisely as possible.

There are several ways to control this. To try them out, open an image and practice getting different views of it.

Zoom

When you open Elements, the long vertical window at the upper left corner of your screen is called the Tool bar. If this is not visible, go to Window>Tools to bring it up.

From the Tool bar, select (by clicking on it) the icon that looks like a magnifying glass (near the bottom right corner). This is called the Zoom tool.

Position it over the area you want to zoom in on and click one or more times. To zoom out, hold down the Alt/Opt key (a little minus sign will appear on the magnifying glass) and click one or more times.

You can also click and drag over the area that you want to appear on your screen. If you click and drag over a small area, it will be greatly enlarged to fill your screen. If you click and drag over a larger area, it will still jump to fill your screen, but it won't be as greatly enlarged.

Percentage View

At the lower-left corner of your document, you'll see the percentage view (below). You can type in any percentage that you like, enlarging or reducing your view of the document accordingly. Just to the right of the percentage view,

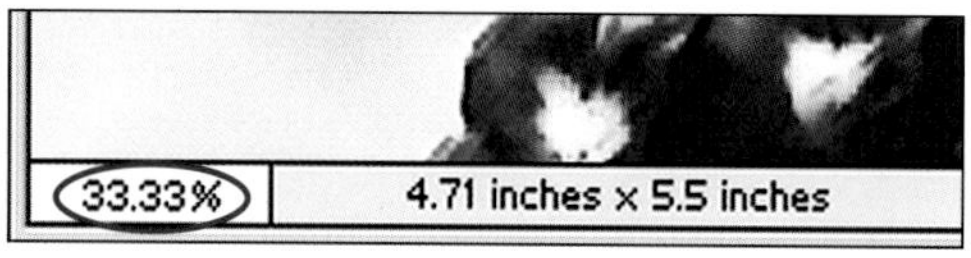

There are several ways to control your image view in Elements. As seen above, you can enter the percentage at which you want to view the image in the lower-left corner of the image window. The Tool bar, from which you can select the Zoom tool to magnify your image, is shown to the right.

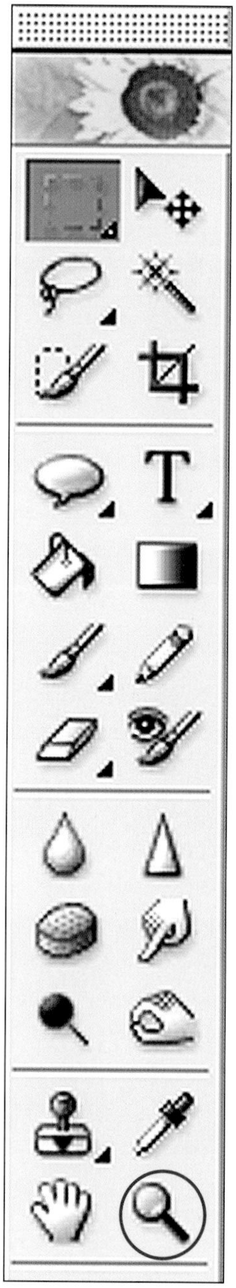

At the top of the View menu, you'll find some options for controlling your image view. The Fit on Screen option is particularly helpful.

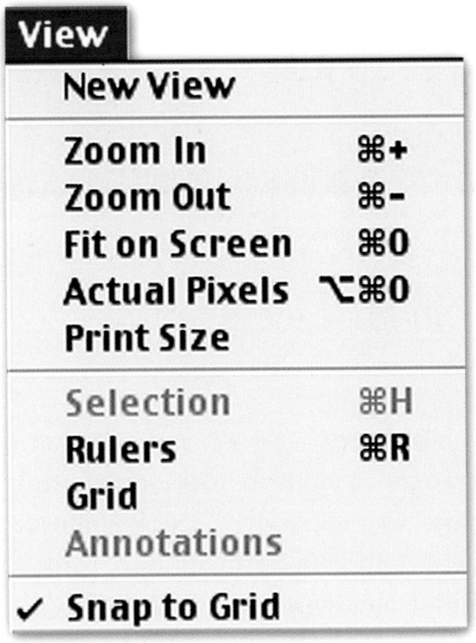

you'll see the dimensions of your image—a handy reminder.

View Menu

At the top of the View menu you'll also find several ways to control your image view. The most useful for beginners are: Zoom In and Zoom Out (like the Zoom tool), and Fit on Screen (a quick way to view your entire image).

Scrolling

Once you have zoomed in, you can use the scroll bars at the right and bottom of the screen to move across the image and view individual areas at a higher magnification.

Navigator

To view the Navigator window, go to Window>Show Navigator.

The percentage at the lower left corner of this window indicates the current view (you can type over it to change this). You can also move the slider at the bottom to the right or left to change the size of the area being viewed. Similarly, clicking on the small mountains zooms out, while clicking on large mountains zooms in.

In the Navigator window, a red box indicates the area that is currently visible on screen. Once you've zoomed in to the desired enlargement, you can simply click and drag the red box over the area that you want to see displayed in your main window.

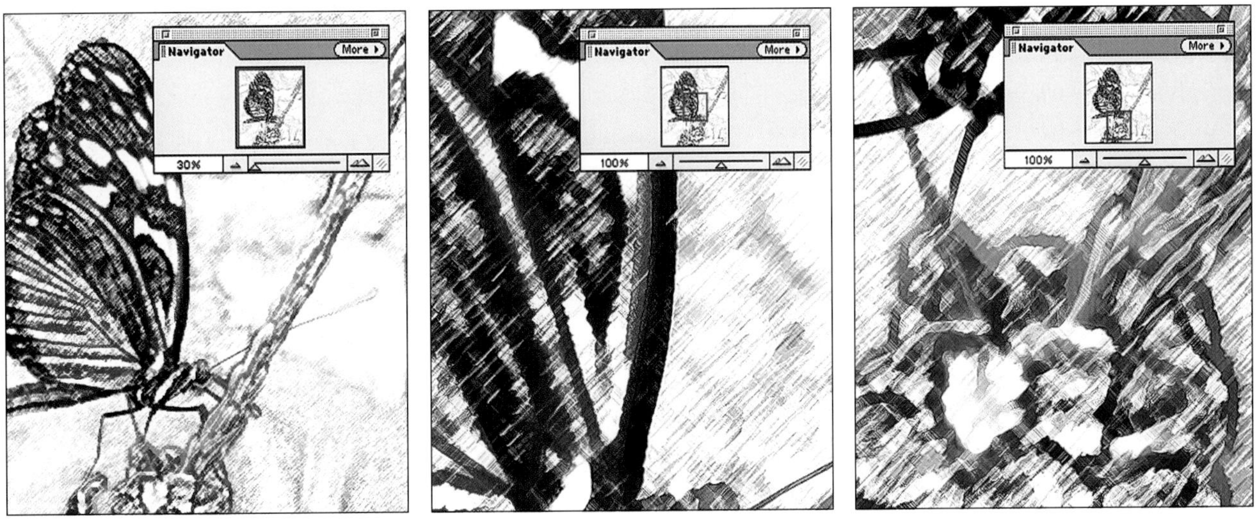

In the Navigator window (shown inset in the above images), the red box indicates the area of the image that is visible on-screen (left). When you zoom in, the visible area is reduced (center). You can click and drag on the red box to change the area of the image that is visible without changing its enlargement (right).

CORRECTING MISTAKES

If there's one thing about digital imaging that really stands out, it's how forgiving it is. When you mess up (and you will mess up), you can backtrack without having to start over from scratch.

Yes, you're going to make mistakes from time to time. You'll apply the wrong effect (or realize that the intended one makes the image look really bad). Here's what to do.

Edit>Undo

If you notice right away that you don't like what you just did, go to Edit>Undo. This will reverse the last thing you did, but *only* the last thing. If you make three brush strokes before noticing you used the wrong color, going to Edit>Undo will only reverse the third stroke; the first and second will remain.

If you go to Edit>Undo, and then immediately return to the Edit pull-down menu, you'll see that the Undo option has changed to Redo. Using Undo and Redo, you can toggle between what the image looked like with and without your last change.

Undo History

Since the Edit>Undo command can only undo the very last thing you did, what happens if you realize you made a terrible mistake three steps back?

The Undo History palette records each change you make to an image. This includes any action that affects the pixels in the image, so it does not include things like zooming in and out, moving palettes around on your screen, etc. It does, however, include each individual brush stroke you might use, and just about anything else you can do to an image. If the Undo History palette is not visible on your desktop, go to Window>Undo History.

In its default setting, the Undo History palette will record only the most recent twenty states (the term for the individual entries in the list of steps in the palette). This helps to save memory, but you can set the number of saved states as high as one hundred by going to Edit>Preferences>General.

In the Undo History palette, states are listed from the top down, so the oldest state of the image is at the top of the

TRY IT OUT

The example on the facing page uses tools that we'll be getting to shortly, but you can try out the Undo History without them. Open an image (see pages 14–15) and go to Filter>Artistic>Watercolor. Hit OK in the window that appears. Then, look at the Undo History palette. You'll see a new state called Watercolor under the state labeled Open. Clicking on the Open state will undo the Watercolor filter; clicking on Watercolor will redo it.

When an image (top left) is opened, the Undo History palette showed this operation ("Open") as the first state (bottom left). As changes are made to an image, you can track them from top to bottom through the Undo History palette (bottom center). In the image shown here, Auto Color Correction and Fill Flash were used to correct the exposure, then the Type tool was applied. The type was repositioned using the Move tool, and some special effects (called Styles) were applied. The resulting image (top center) was okay, but I wanted to see it again without the type. To do this, I simply clicked on the history state above the Type-tool state (right bottom). This cleared the type and all the effects (top right). I could begin working from here and automatically delete all the following states, or return to any other state and continue working from there.

list, and the newest one is at the bottom. Each state is listed with the name of the tool or command used to create it, so you can navigate back through the history of an image pretty easily when you need to backtrack.

By clicking on the states in this timeline, you can move back and forth through the history of the image and compare previous versions to the current one, or to undo the last ten steps.

When you select a state, you'll see that the ones below it dim. This indicates that if you continue working from the selected state, these later states will be discarded. Similarly, deleting a state (by dragging it into the trash can at the bottom of the palette) will discard all the states that came after it.

If you accidentally eliminate a set of states you wanted to keep, immediately go to Edit>Undo to restore them.

When you close an image, all of the saved states will be deleted, so be sure you're done with them before you close the image!

CHANGING IMAGE SIZE

Making an 8x10-inch print? A 4x6-inch print? A T-shirt? A greeting card? All of the above? In most cases, you'll want to adjust the size of your image to suit your final purposes for it.

More often than not, your image won't be exactly the size you want it for your print (or greeting card, or T-shirt, or web site, etc.). In these cases, you'll need to change the image size. If your image will be used in several ways, you may need to resize a few times to get the assortment of sizes you need. Whenever you resize, remember to work from your largest needed file to your smallest. As noted on pages 6–7, Elements does a much better job at removing pixels than adding them, so this will help to ensure that your image quality remains as high as possible.

Image Size

Going to Image>Resize>Image Size lets you enter a height, width, and resolution for your image.

At the bottom of the Image Size window, you'll see two very important

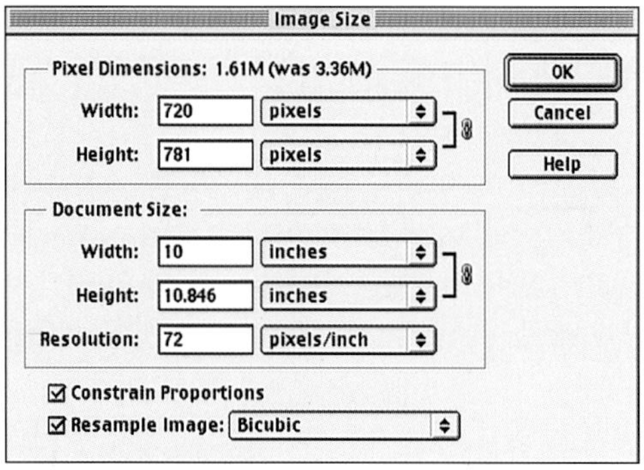

The Image Size window.

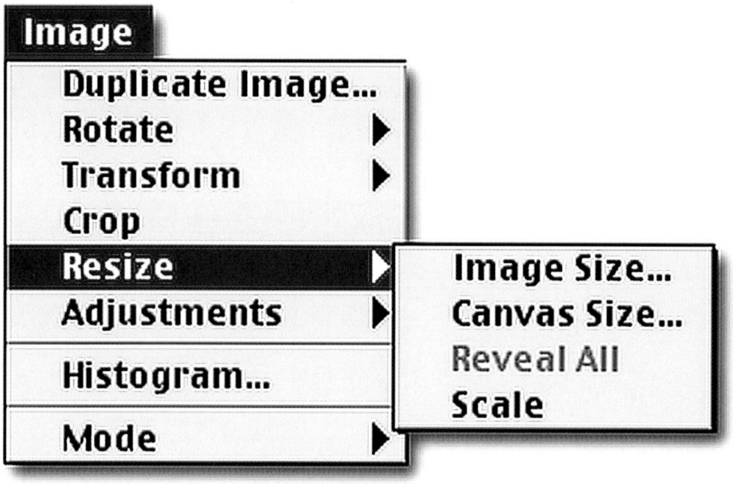

The Image menu contains options for resizing your photographs.

boxes. This first is the Constrain Proportions box. When this is checked, the original relationship between the height and width of the image will be retained. Unless you intend to distort your photograph, you should always keep this box checked.

The Resample Image box lets you tell Elements whether you want it to add or subtract from the total number of pixels in your image. If this box *is not* checked, increasing the height and width of your image will decrease the resolution (the existing pixels will be spread out over a greater area). If this box *is* checked, increasing the height and width of your image will not change the resolution (more pixels will be created to fill the greater area).

Canvas Size

Going to Image>Resize>Canvas Size lets you enter additional height and/or width around your image. The color of this extra space will be determined by the background color (see pages 98–99). This is a good way to create extra space around a photograph. You can then use the space to add text or other image elements.

In the Canvas Size window, the current width and height of your image are displayed at the top. You can then enter the desired new size and width below that. Pull-down menus let you select your preferred unit of measurement.

At the bottom of the box you can select an anchor position. This determines where the new canvas area will be added around your image. If you leave the anchor (indicated by the dark gray box) in the center of the grid, the new canvas will be added equally around all side of your image. If you anchor your image at the bottom left, the new canvas will be added above and to the right of the image.

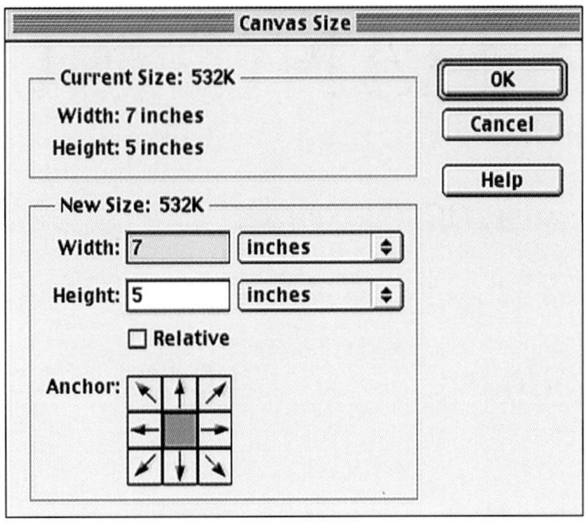

The Canvas Size window.

Scale

Going to Image>Resize>Scale lets you resize your image by clicking and dragging on a bounding box. This technique is covered in detail on pages 34–35, where you'll learn how to accomplish several similar transformations.

Increasing the canvas size gives you room to add text around an image.

SAVING IMAGES

This might sound like a trivial topic—until the first time you look for an image and can't find it. Saving your images wisely makes it easy to retrieve them and can help optimize them for Internet use.

To save a new image, go to File> Save. The Save As window will then appear. In it, you can set the destination for your new file, enter the name of the file, and select a file format. Then hit OK. With some file formats, a second window will appear—often offering you compression options. Set these as you like. After you have saved a file once, going to File>Save will update that same file with any changes you have made (no window will appear).

Making a Backup

When you are working with digital images, especially those from a digital camera, your original file is essentially your negative—the image as you shot it. One of the marvelous things about digital imaging is that you can mess around

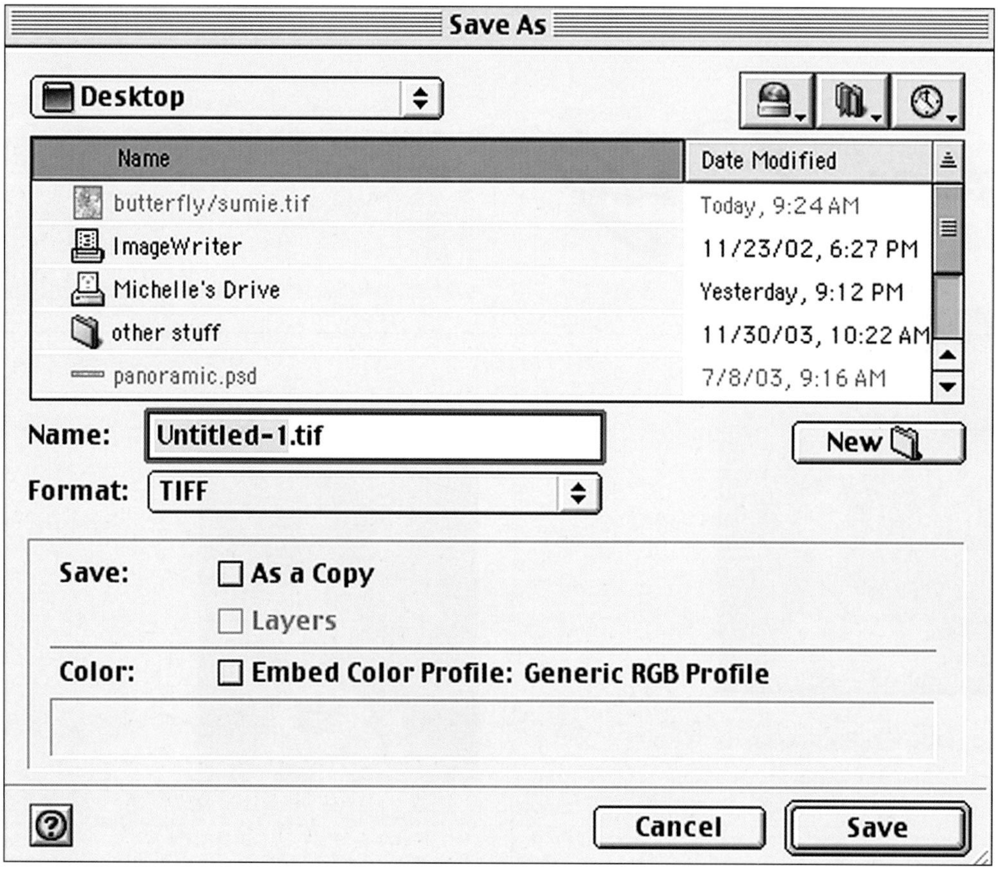

The Save As window lets you specify the location where you want your image saved (from the pull-down menu at the top of the window). Type the name you'd like for your image in the Name field, and select the desired file format from the Format pull-down menu. You can also choose to save the file as a copy (good for making backups) or to preserve layers in the image (see page 83). Advanced users can also imbed a color profile for their monitor.

In the Save for Web window, the image on the left is your original, and the one on the right is a preview of the image optimized for the web. Beneath the preview, you can see the total size of the file and the approximate time it will take to load. On the right-hand side of the window, you can adjust the settings to maximize the appearance of the image while minimizing its load time.

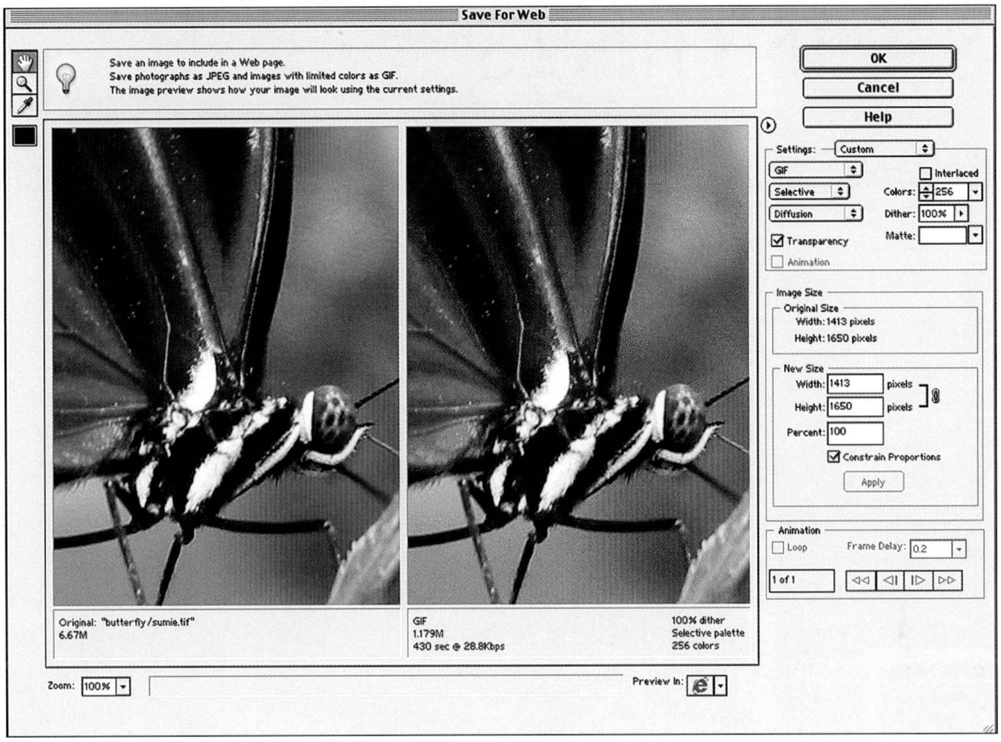

with an image today, and tomorrow (when you decide your grandmother might not find it all that funny to see her head on a monkey), you can just start over from the original file.

For this reason, it's important to make backups of your original images. Ideally, you'll probably want to burn these unaltered images to CD or DVD, ensuring that you won't be able to accidentally save over them and destroy your original.

At the very least, when you start work on a new image, you should save it as a copy. You can do this by going to File>Save As and checking the "As a Copy" box near the bottom of the window, or simply by selecting a new file name (like "Grandma_backup.tif" or "beachshot_inprogress.tif").

Save for Web

To save an image to use on the Internet (on a web site or as an e-mail attachment), go to File>Save for Web. From the dialog box, you can select settings and see how long an image will take to load on a viewer's screen, as well as how it will look. You can even preview the image in Microsoft® Internet Explorer® or Netscape® Communicator®.

SAVING FOR THE INTERNET

When saving images for use on the Internet, you need to consider image quality (how good the image looks on screen) and load time (how long it takes to appear on your screen). Typically, load times are reduced by eliminating data—and this reduces the visual quality of the image. There's no one setting that will work with every photo, but if you spend a few seconds playing with the settings in the Save for Web window, you can almost always improve your load time without making too big a sacrifice in image quality.

CHAPTER THREE

Hints, Help, and Recipes

If ever there was a user-friendly imaging program, it's Elements. Throughout the user interface, you'll find tips, tricks, and quick access to help files that are actually easy to understand.

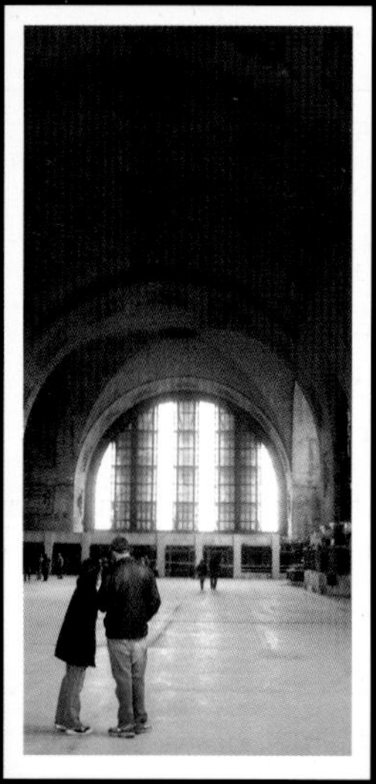

HINTS

The Hints palette can really expand your knowledge of Elements. It's a great resource when you're trying to figure out how to use a new tool or menu item.

Elements offers users a variety of very powerful imaging tools, menus, and options. As a result, you'll probably find (at least from time to time) that you've forgotten what a particular one does, or you can't remember how to adjust a particular setting to get the effect you want—or you might even find yourself totally puzzled as to why something doesn't seem to be working as you thought it would. While it's easy to get frustrated, help is actually only a click away.

Hints

A great resource to take advantage of when using Elements is the Hints palette. If this is not visible on your screen, go to Window>Hints to bring it up. Although this palette appears by default as a free-floating window, once you've worked with Elements for a while, you may find it preferable to drag this palette into the palette well. It's something you'll refer to only periodically once you get the hang of the tools, so you'll probably want to devote your

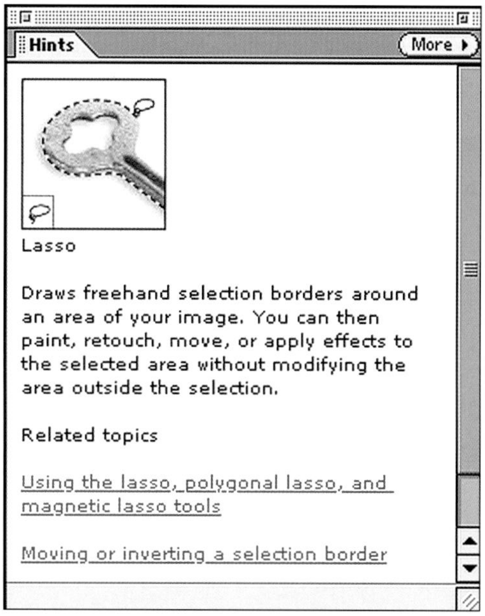

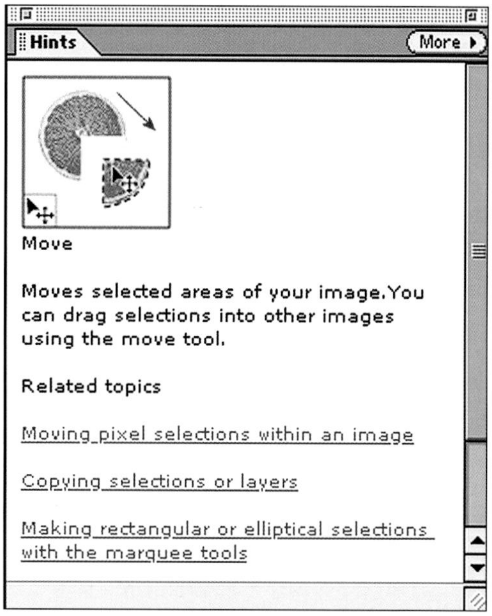

The Hints palette displays displays information for the currently active tool or menu option (the tool or menu option you've clicked on). It gives you an overview of what the tool does, and links you to additional information in the help files.

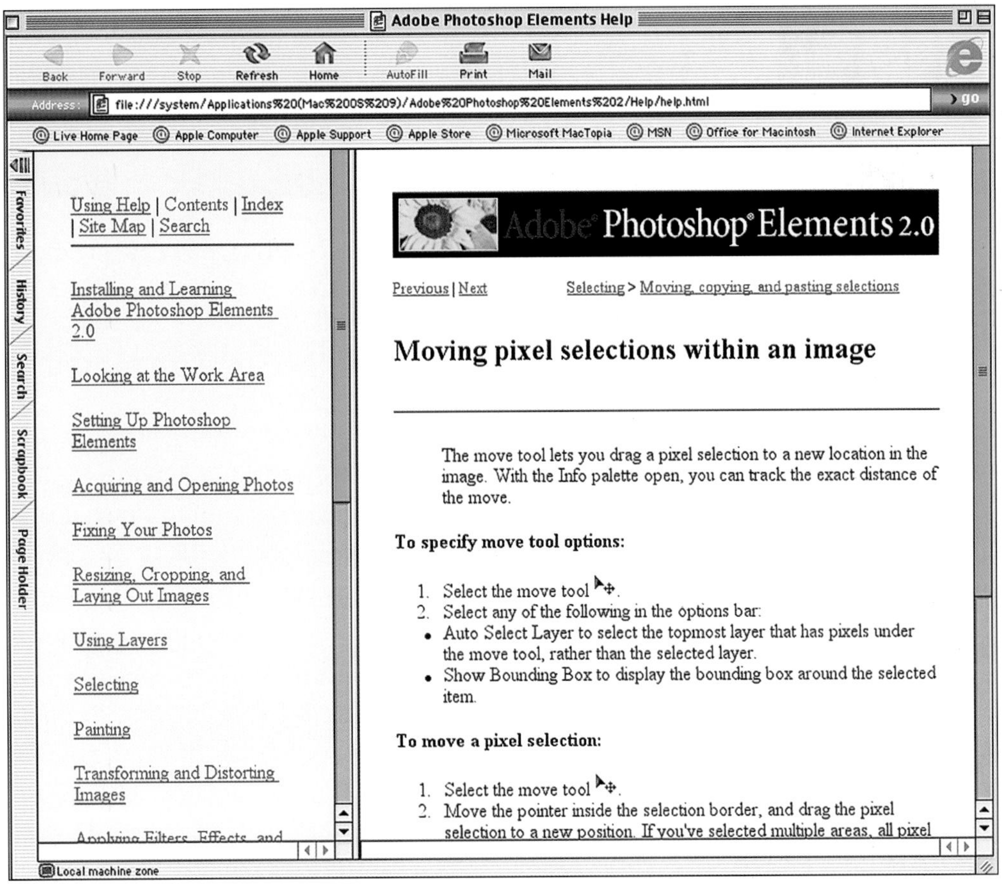

Clicking on any of the "related topics" links at the bottom of the Hints palette will open your web browser and the full Elements help files.

limited screen space to palettes you need to refer to more often.

If you open the Hints palette on your screen and click on one of the tools in the Tool bar (see page 13), you'll notice that the name of that tool and a description of its function appears in the Hints palette. This information will change for every tool and menu item, making it a great resource for refreshing your memory about these items.

Related Topics

Below the description of the tool or menu-item function, you'll see a section called "related topics." Under this heading, you'll find hyperlinks (the blue underlined text) to files in the full Elements help files. If you click on any of these links, your web browser will open and the requested entry will be displayed. These entries are usually extremely detailed and are almost sure to answer just about any question you might have. Be prepared, however, to look under more than one entry, since sometimes the answer won't be filed quite where you'd first think to look for it.

For more information on using the help files, turn to the next page.

HELP

The help files in Elements can be your best friend when trying to tackle a tricky problem or locate a setting that you rarely need to access. They may even provide you with some new ideas.

While digital imaging is a tremendously exciting and powerful tool for photographers, there's no denying that the learning curve is steep. The help files are a great resource wherever you are on that curve, providing exhaustive information that covers everything from the most basic concepts to the minute details of tool options and program preferences.

Accessing Help

As noted on pages 26–27, one of the ways to access the help files is to click on the tool or menu option about which you have a question and look at the Hints palette.

If your question isn't as much about a tool as about a concept or an operation, you might want to use the search option on the Shortcuts bar instead. To do this, just enter the term or terms you want to look for and hit Search. This will open the Search Results window and give you a list of some topics that match your search. Locate the one that seems most appropriate and click on the question mark next to it. This will launch your web browser and the full version of the Elements help files.

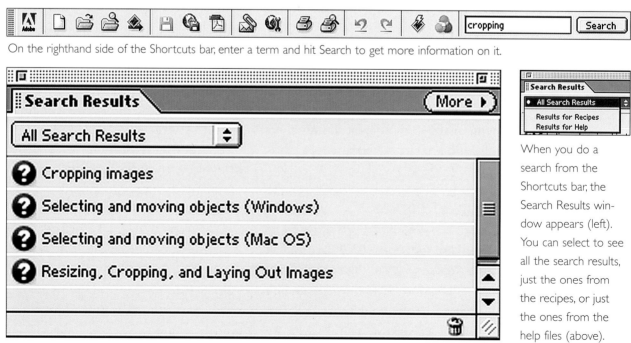

On the righthand side of the Shortcuts bar, enter a term and hit Search to get more information on it.

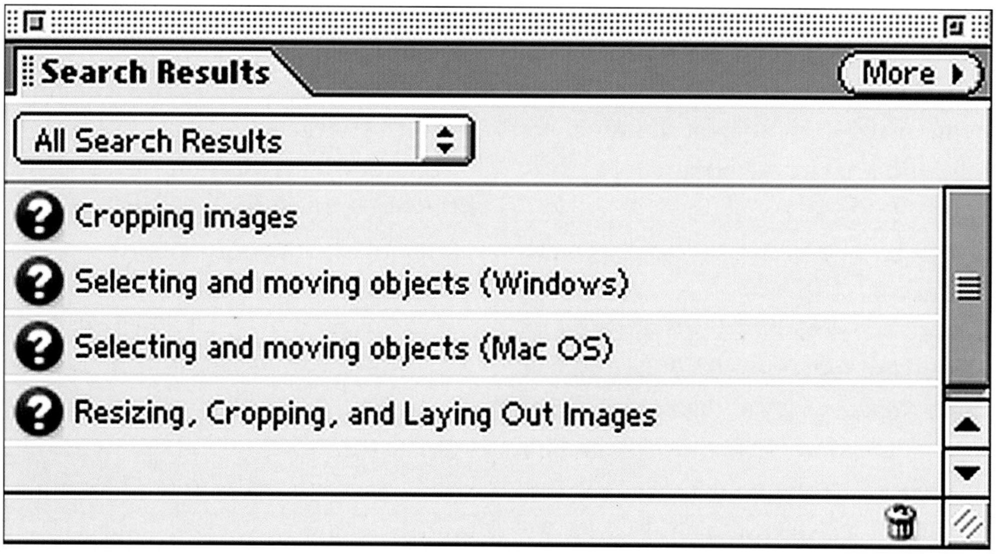

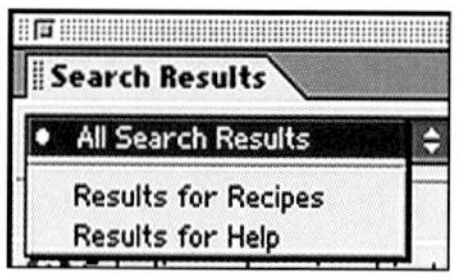

When you do a search from the Shortcuts bar, the Search Results window appears (left). You can select to see all the search results, just the ones from the recipes, or just the ones from the help files (above).

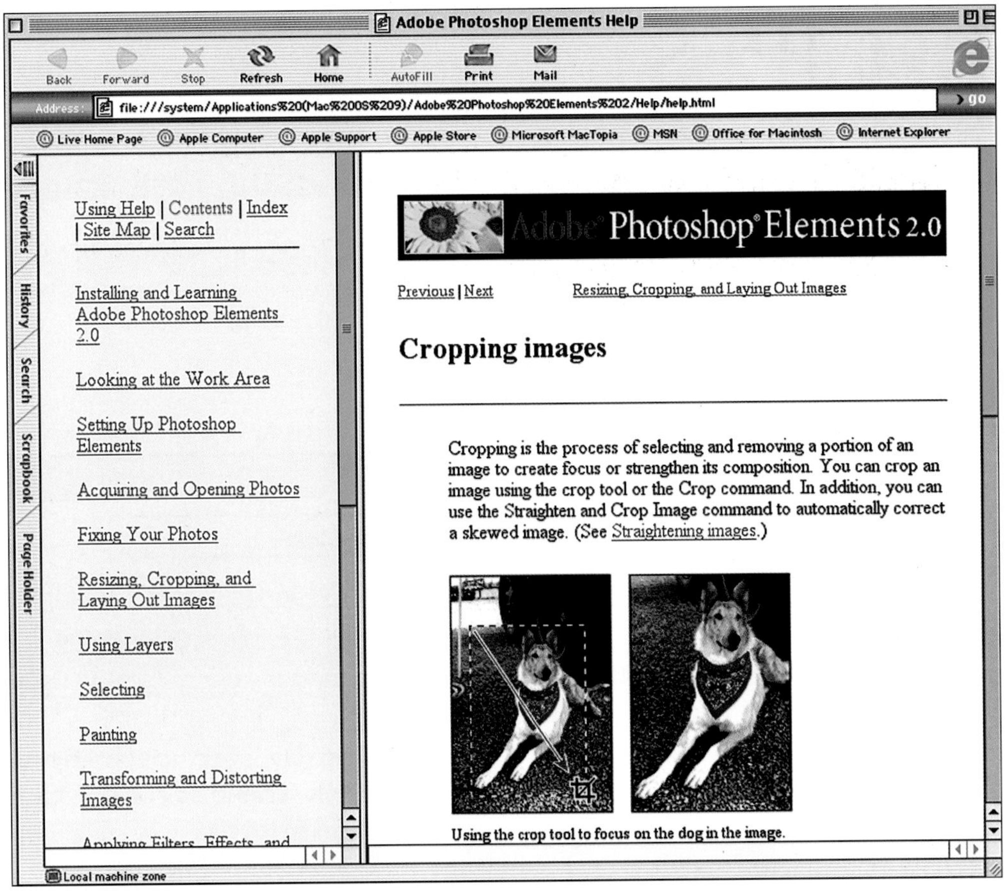

The Elements help files are viewed in your web browser.

To go directly to the full help files, you can also hit the question-mark shortcut just to the left of the Palette well (see page 12).

Alternately, you can go to Help> Photoshop Elements Help. From the Help menu, you can also access an alphabetized glossary of terms useful for users of Elements, online tutorials, and online updates for your software.

Using Help

If you get to the help files via the Hints palette or a Shortcuts-bar search, you'll already have narrowed down the topic that will be displayed. If you hit the question-mark shortcut or open the help files from the Window menu, you'll need to perform a search for the topic you need information on.

To do this, look to the top left corner of the screen (this column is called the navigation frame) and hit Search. A new page will load with a window at the top left. Type your search terms into this window and hit Search. Select an entry from the text that appears under the search box, and the information will appear to the right (called the topic frame). Additional related links will be listed at the bottom off the topic frame, so be sure to scroll down to them—especially if the text in the frame hasn't quite answered your question.

You may also find it useful to take advantage of the site index; just hit the link at the top of the navigation frame to access this. This can sometimes remind you of related topics that will help you refine your search.

RECIPES

Using the image-enhancement recipes in the How To palette is a great way to see the power of Elements in action—and an easy way to accomplish some common tasks.

The recipes found in the How To palette are step-by-step instruction for accomplishing a wide range of common imaging tasks.

To open this palette go to Window> How To. You can leave this palette in the Palette Well or (if you find that you tend to use it a lot) drag it onto the desktop to turn it into a free-floating window.

Using Recipes

To use a recipe, open the How To palette and select one of the categories from the Select a Recipe pull-down menu at the top of the palette. When you do this, the list of recipes in that category will appear and you can pick the one that seems to best suit your needs. You can also preview the steps before starting to make sure you know how to do everything.

Some of the recipes contain techniques that will de difficult to do until you've finished reading this book. Others are very simple—using the red-eye removal recipe under the retouching header, for example, probably won't be too hard for most beginners. For now, just keep these recipes in mind, and know that they are there to help you in a pinch!

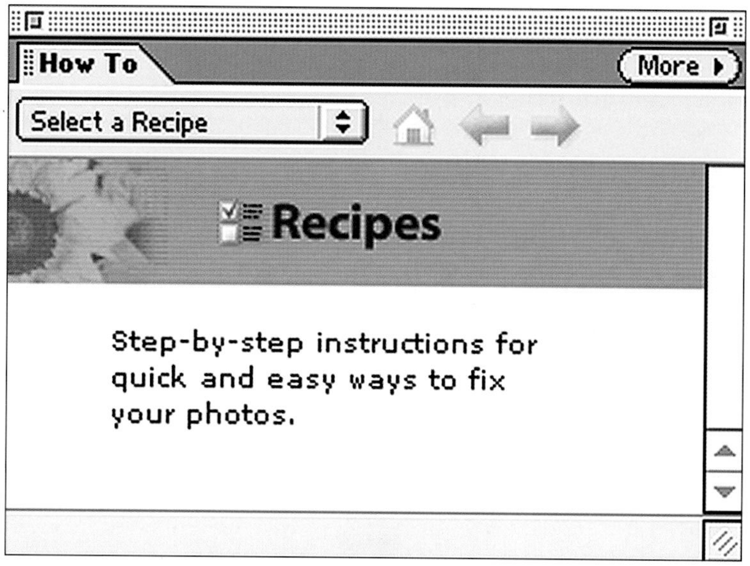

To view the recipes, go to Window> How To.

Getting New Recipes

From the Select-a-Recipe menu in the How To palette, you can also select to download new recipes from the Adobe web site. If you like using the recipes, this is a great way to expand your abilities and add some new functionality to your Elements software. To access this feature, simply click on it in the How To palette pull-down window while you are online. Adobe updates these files regularly, so check back from time to time for the latest materials.

Let's look at an example, using the recipes to fix a dark and poorly color-balanced image.

1 Open an image in Elements. This image is dark and the color doesn't look good.

2 At the top of the How To palette, select Fix Color and Brightness. From the menu that appears, select Lighten Dark Areas of a Photo.

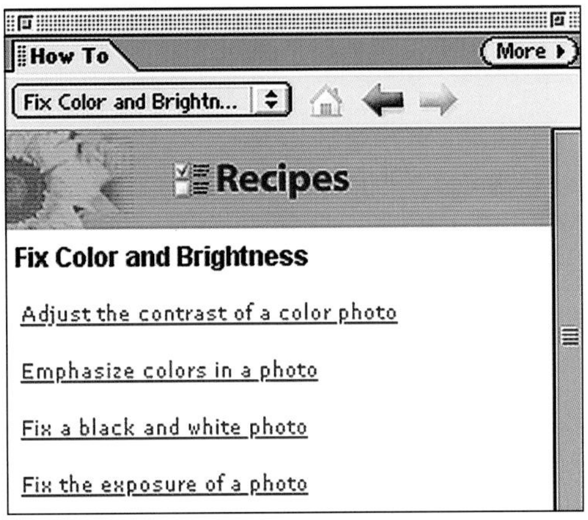

3 The recipe for lightening dark areas appears. For some steps in a recipe (in this case, the first step) you can have Elements do some of the work for you. Then, follow along with the rest of the steps, using your own judgment to adjust the settings as needed.

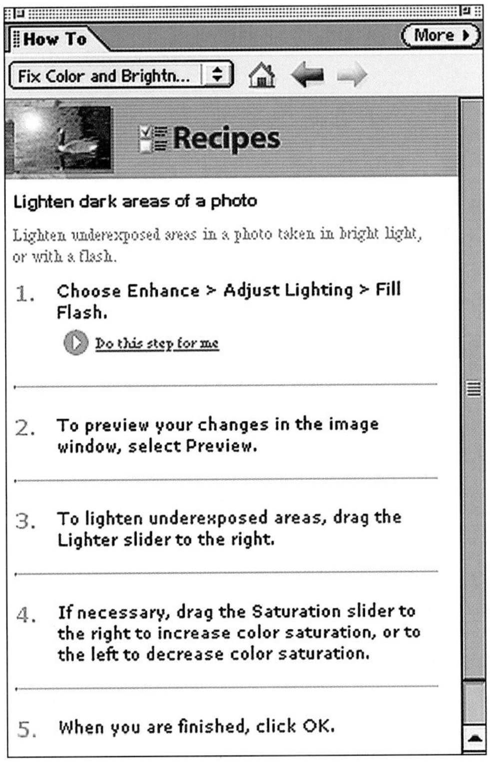

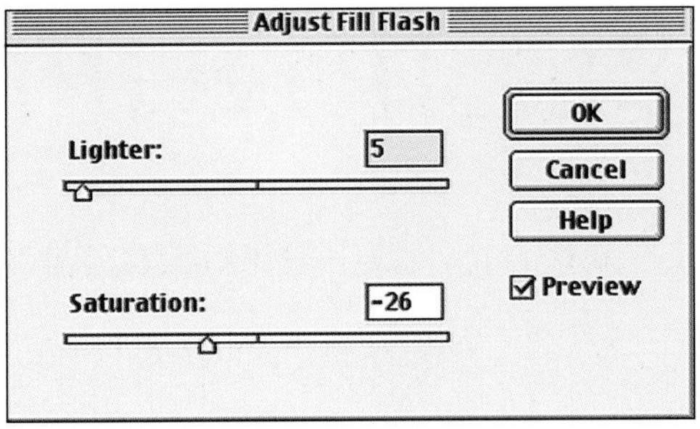

4 In the Adjust Fill Flash dialog box, the settings were adjusted until the exposure looked better. It still wasn't quite right though, so the Remove a Color Cast option (under Fix Color and Brightness) was selected from the recipes. (When viewing the steps in a recipe, you can get back to the main menu category—here, Fix Color and Brightness—by hitting the house or back-arrow button at the top of the How To palette.)

5 Taking care of the exposure problem and the color cast using the recipes worked quite well—the final image definitely looks much better. You could use it as is or continue to make additional adjustments.

Be[illegible] you get started wo[illegible]g on an image, you'll often need to rotate it, crop it, or even adjust for perspective problems. These are quick procedures when you are using Elements.

DUPLICATE, ROTATE

These are some very basic operations—but they are so common that you'll probably use one or both of them on almost every image you work with.

If you've just scanned an image or just imported an image from your digital camera, it's an extremely good idea to make a duplicate of the original before you begin manipulating it in Elements. You may think you won't make any mistakes—but, like the rest of us, sooner or later you will. And when that mistake is accidentally saving an edited version of an image over the one and only original, it can be pretty frustrating—especially if you wanted to try some other effects on that original before deciding which you liked best.

Duplicate

To quickly make a backup of your image, you can simply go to Image> Duplicate Image. In the box that appears, you can rename your duplicated image, or use the suggested name (which will be your current file name plus the word "copy"). When you hit the OK button, a duplicate image window will appear in the Elements workspace. This will be the copy of your original image, and you can begin working on this copy without altering your original. This procedure also works well when you are in the process of working on an image and want to compare before and afters side by side. Just duplicate the "before" image, make your change on the copy, then position the images side by side on your screen and decide which one you like the best.

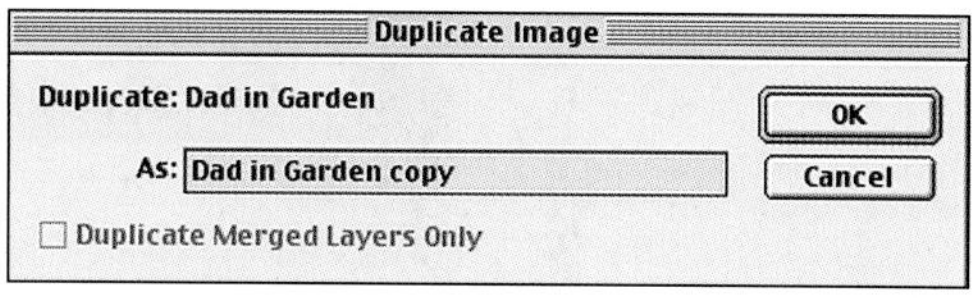

In the Duplicate Image box you can rename the new image, or leave the suggested name (your original image name plus "copy") in place.

Rotate Image

Under Image>Rotate, the top portion of the drop-down menu contains options for rotating your image. When you shoot with a digital camera, this is the function you'll use to properly orient your vertical images (the ones shot with

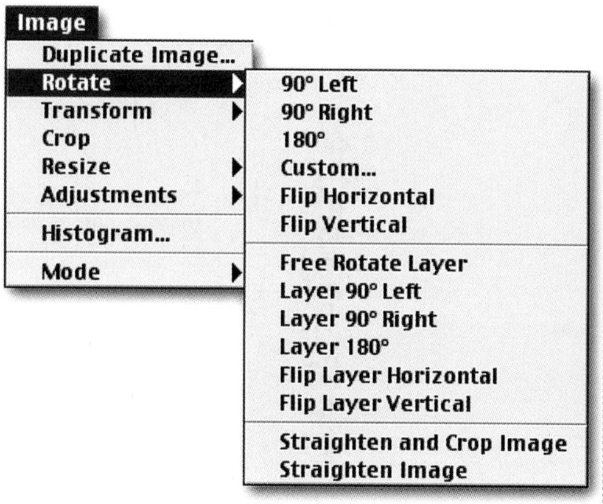

Under the Image menu, you can duplicate or rotate your image.

To take a vertical photo, you tilt your digital camera. When these images are transferred to your computer, they will appear as horizontals, though (above). To get the proper orientation, just rotate them 90 degrees to the left or right (right).

the camera turned on its side). Depending on the image, you can decide whether it needs to be rotated 90 degrees left or right. You can also rotate it 180 degrees—useful if you scanned it upside down (or shot it upside down during your trapeze lesson). You can also rotate image layers (see chapter 8).

There are some other options for rotating your images—but you probably won't use these quite as often. First, you can select Image>Rotate>Custom and select a specific angle to which you want the image rotated. Extra blank space will be added around your image to accommodate this rotation, and its color will

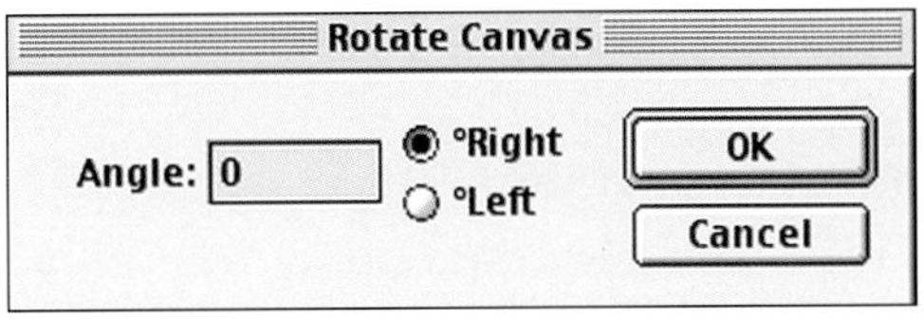

Enter the angle to which you want to rotate the image, note whether it is to the left or right, then hit OK to rotate.

be the color you have set for the background color (see pages 98–99).

You can also flip your images horizontally or vertically. This can be useful when scanning slides or negatives, which are easy to flip the wrong way in the scanner.

Straighten and Crop Image

At the bottom of the Rotate pull-down menu, you can select Straighten and Crop Image or Straighten Image. As the name suggests, these options are designed to automatically crop out extraneous material and correct any perspective problems in your images. With some images, these functions actually work pretty well; with others, they fall well short of the mark. On the next few pages, we'll look at some more precise and controlled ways to accomplish these same tasks in precisely the way you want them for your individual image.

TRANSFORMATIONS

With architectural subjects in particular, photographing from an angle (like looking up at a tall building) causes some distortion. Eliminating this gives your photos a more professional look.

When photographing a subject with strong geometric lines, you get the best results when you keep your camera square to the subject—but sometimes this isn't feasible. For example, unless you have an extreme wide-angle lens or can shoot from far away, you normally can't keep your camera square to the subject when photographing a tall building from the ground. This sort of distortion is such a common problem among photographers that Elements has some special tools to help fix it (and to create some other interesting effects, if you like). These are found under Image>Transform.

Getting Started

Transforms can be done to layers (see chapter 8) or selections (see chapter 9). For now, before applying any of the following effects, go to Select>All. You will see a blinking dotted line appear around your entire image, indicating that the changes you make will apply to the entire image. For this reason, you should strongly consider working on a duplicate file (see page 32). When you've moved on to learn about layers and selections, you can use them when applying transforms—but this will give you a feel for the process.

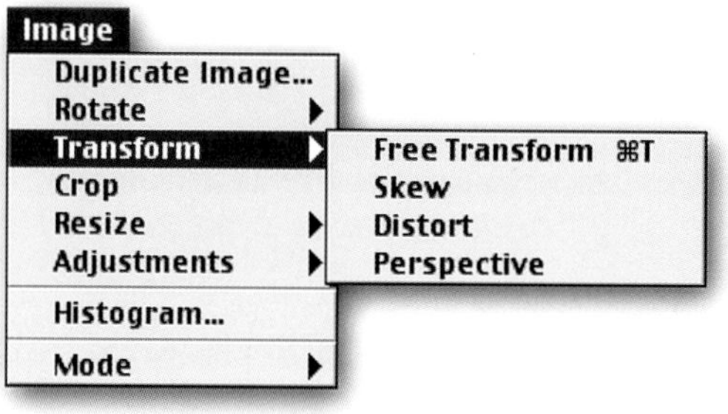

From the Image>Transform pull-down menu, you can select several types of transformations.

The Basics of Transforms

When you select any of the options from this pull-down list, an indicator box with handles (the small boxes at each corner and in the centers of the sides) will appear over your image. If you can't see the edges of your image, reduce your view of the image until you can see your whole image and some gray area around it (see pages 18–19). By clicking and dragging on these handles, you will manipulate the image data within the frame of the photograph. Which option you select from the Transform pull-down menu will dictate how you will be allowed to move the handles.

Free Transform

When you select this option, you will be able to move the sides, top, and bottom of the image in or out and up or down.

The photo on the left was taken from slightly below and to the left of the window. As a result, the vertical and horizontal lines are all slightly skewed and the window seems distorted. Going to Image>Transform>Distort allowed the image to actually be "undistorted"—resulting in a much better-looking image (right).

Skew

With this option selected, the handles will move only in a straight line in a given direction.

Distort

With the Distort function selected, all of the handles will move freely in every direction.

Perspective

When you select Perspective, the changes you make are mirrored top to bottom and/or left to right. For example, if you move the bottom-left handle in toward the center of the image, the bottom right handle will also move an equal distance in toward the center of the image. This is a good choice for images where your camera was only tilted in one direction (like up toward a tall building).

Accept or Decline

Hit Return to accept the change. If you want to use more than one selection from the Transform menu, you can just choose it without first accepting the existing change (i.e., you can switch back and forth, then click OK to apply the cumulative changes). If you don't like the change, click on another tool from the Tool bar and cancel the transformation when prompted.

CROPPING

One of the quickest ways to improve the look of many images is by cropping out areas that distract the viewer from your subject. Cropping also changes the image size, though, so it needs be done carefully.

The Crop tool (see page 13) is used to remove extraneous areas from the edges of a photo. This is a great way to improve the look of photographs you didn't have time to frame carefully or ones that you just didn't compose as well as you might have liked.

To crop an image, choose the Crop tool from the Tool bar. Click and drag over the area of your image that you want to keep, then release your mouse button. You don't have to be incredibly precise. At each corner of the crop indicator (the dotted line) you will see small boxes. These are handles that you can click and drag to reshape or reposition the box. (As you get near the edges of the photo, these handles tend to "stick" to the edges. To prevent this, click on the handle you want to drag, then press and hold the Control key while moving the handle.) When the cropped area looks right, hit Enter.

Straightening Images

The Crop tool can also be used very effectively to straighten a crooked image. Simply click and drag over the image with the Crop tool, then position your mouse over one of the corner han-

Cropping is a great way to eliminate distractions from an image.

Cropping is a quick way to straighten out a crooked image, but you do lose some pixels in the process. Here, it's not a problem, but it could be more of an issue in other photos.

dles until the cursor's arrow icon turns into a bent arrow icon. Once you see this, click and rotate the crop indicator as needed. Doing this may cause the edges of the box that indicates the crop area to go outside the edges of the image. If this happens, simply click and drag on each one to reposition them inside the frame.

Crop Tool Options

In the Options bar at the top of the screen you can set the final size of the cropped image. This is helpful if, for instance, you specifically want to create a 4"x6" print to frame. Simply enter the desired height, width, and resolution needed before cropping, then click and drag over the image to select just the area you want in your print. The Crop tool will automatically constrain itself to the desired proportions.

Also in the Options bar is a setting for the shield color and opacity. This shield obscures the area you are cropping out, giving you a better idea of what the photo will look like with these areas removed. Leaving it set to black will usually be fine, but you can change the color by clicking on the rectangle to the right of the words Shield Color. You can also adjust the opacity to allow the cropped-out area to be partially visible. To turn off the shield, uncheck the box to the left of Shield Color.

Select to Crop

You can also use any of the selection tools (see pages 90–93) to crop an image. To do this, select any area of the image, then, with the selection still active, go to Image>Crop.

CROPPING AND RESOLUTION

Cropping reduces the total number of pixels in an image. If you are scanning an image and plan to crop it, you may therefore wish to scan your image at a higher resolution or enlargement to compensate for this reduction. If you are working with an image from a digital camera, the total number of pixels in your image is fixed, so you'll need to determine the final resolution and image size you need and not crop the image to a smaller size than that.

CHAPTER FIVE

Color and Exposure

Most images can benefit from at least a little tweaking of their color and exposure—after all, now that the control is in your hands (instead of the lab's) why not strive for perfection?

ADJUSTING COLOR

Making color look right is challenging, but it's probably the most important thing you can do to make your images look their very best.

As people who see color all around us every day, we are very savvy about color—we know how things are supposed to look, and when they aren't right, we notice it. Even if we don't know exactly what the problem is, we still see it. The following are some of the challenges to be aware of as you begin working with digital color.

Color is Subjective

Color is subjective. As a fact of biology, our eyes actively work to preserve the appearance of object colors in changing light, to enhance color differences between objects and their surroundings, and to inform our perception of color using our memories of what objects look like. While this is a marvelous thing in terms of survival (differentiating poisonous berries from ones that are safe to eat, seeing the green snake hiding in the foliage up ahead, etc.), it makes things tricky for people concerned with reproducing colors accurately.

Color Vision

Evolution has decided for us that as the brain sorts through the data it receives from the eyes, it should try to standardize it in order to give us the best possible information by which to survive. As a result of this, blue objects always look blue—whether we see them under fluorescent, natural, or incandescent light. This is because we don't determine the color of an object in isolation—our perception of one color is linked to our perception of the colors around it.

You can experiment with this by turning on an incandescent light in a room that has previously been lit only by the sun. At first, the light from the bulb will look pretty orange. But gradually, your eyes will compensate for this and it will begin to look white.

Luminous Sources

When we look at a source of light, our eyes are constantly adjusting to it. That

JUST WALK AWAY

Sometimes you'll reach a point where you aren't sure if your corrections are helping at all. When this happens, it helps to walk away for a little while and relax your eyes. When you return to your image, you'll often be able to see immediately what steps are needed to make it look better.

means that the longer you stare at your image on the monitor, the better it sometimes looks. This can make you think it's okay when it's not. The luminous monitor also makes our pupils close down, which can lead us to think an image is darker than it really is. (For more objective information on your images, try using the Eyedropper tool, discussed on pages 54–55.)

Viewing Area

Your eyes will adapt to your monitor no matter what you do, but taking control of your viewing environment can help. Start by selecting a neutral gray for your computer's desktop pattern, since the colors you see *around* the edges of an image can affect how you perceive the colors *in* the image. The color of the environment around the monitor can also cast color reflections onto it, so try to keep the area neutral and constant. If possible, place your computer in a room with white or gray walls and position it so that there is no glare on the screen. Wear dark, neutral-colored clothing when working on color-sensitive projects, and try to keep the light levels (and types) in the room constant throughout the day, and from day to day.

Even relatively small variations in color can make a big difference in a photograph—especially where skin tones are concerned.

AUTOMATIC CORRECTIONS

It may sound too good to be true. Can a single operation really make your images look that much better? Sometimes yes, sometimes no—but it's almost always worth a try!

If you've ever had the experience of developing or printing either color or black & white images in a traditional darkroom, you know that getting the tones in your images just right can be a laborious task. With the automatic image-correction functions in Elements, however, it's amazingly simple to create dramatic improvements.

That's the good news. The bad news is that Elements is, after all, a piece of software—it's not equipped with human vision. To compensate for this shortcoming when making its automatic corrections, it is therefore forced to assume what the image is supposed to look like.

Elements assumes, for instance, that you want there to be at least a small very dark area and a small very light area. This is, in general, characteristic of a well-exposed image with good contrast. If you are working with a softly lit photo of a tree in dense fog, however, this assumption isn't going to make your image look very good at all.

The software also makes assumptions about the overall lightness and darkness that an image should have and about how the colors in the image should be balanced. When your images match these assumptions (and many photos actually do—they didn't pull these assumptions out of midair, after all), you are likely to get pretty good results—maybe even great ones—from the auto functions. When your photos don't match these assumptions, however, the results achieved with the auto functions can be pretty scary.

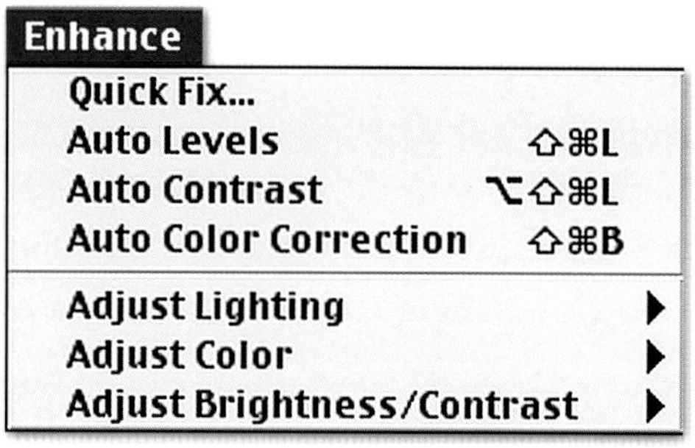

Go to the Enhance pull-down menu to access the auto correction features.

That said, it only takes a couple of seconds to figure out if these methods will give you the results you want, so it's almost always worth giving them a try. Just be prepared to hit Edit>Undo if you aren't happy with the results.

Auto Contrast

The Auto Contrast command, as the name implies, adjusts the contrast of your image—and only the contrast. It will not help any color problems that might be present in your photograph. If the contrast in the image you are working with seems a little flat or dull but the color looks okay, this would be one strategy you could try.

The original photo (top left) lacked contrast and had a yellow color cast. The Auto Contrast (top right) helped the contrast but not the color. The Auto Levels (bottom left) improved both the color and contrast, taking the image to a sepia tone that is probably close to what it originally looked like. The Auto Color Correction (bottom right) fixed the contrast and eliminated the color cast, rendering the photo in pure black & white tones.

Auto Levels

Auto Levels performs a correction that is similar to Auto Contrast, except that it also affects the color of your image. Theoretically, this should remove any overall color cast—but if your image doesn't have an overall color cast, it might actually add one. Still this is worth a try for images that need a little more contrast and have an obvious color cast you want to remove.

Auto Color Correction

This is the most sophisticated of the three automatic functions—and it works remarkably well on a lot of images. While it sometimes introduces color problems, in many images it will be all you need to get the color and contrast to a point that is quite acceptable.

QUICK FIX

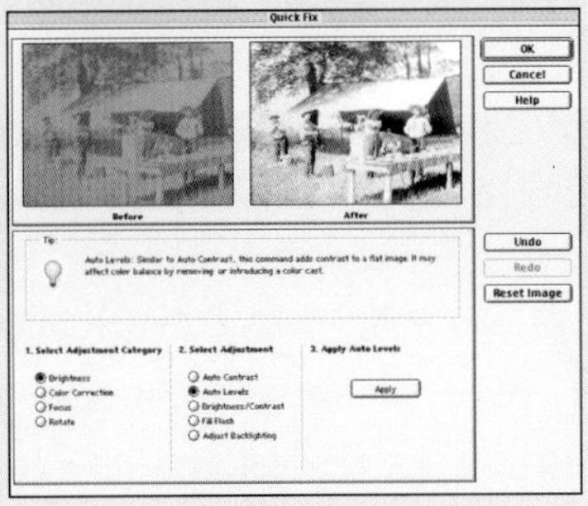

Quick Fix (Enhance>Quick Fix) gives you one-stop access to a number of image-enhancement tools. When you open Quick Fix, a window will open (left) with your original image on the left and your updated image on the right. Use the menus at the bottom of the window to make changes, and hit OK to apply them.

ADJUST LIGHTING

When pros take pictures, they have lighting equipment to perfect each image. For the rest of us, adjusting problematic lighting after the fact can help our images live up to the same high standards.

Elements offers two tools that are designed to help photographers fix a common problem: backlighting.

Backlighting is the term for light that comes from behind the subject of the photograph and toward the photographer. This type of lighting causes two exposure problems. First, the background (where the light is strongest) will be overexposed. It will usually lack detail and be too light. Second, the form of the subject will be in shadow, resulting in skin tones that are too dark.

The best solution for this is to use flash (if your camera has a fill-flash setting, this is what it was designed for) to add light on the subject's face when taking the picture. When this is not possible, though, you can use the Adjust Backlighting and Fill Flash commands to help create a more pleasing image.

It should be noted, however, that you'll get the best results with these tools when they are used on images where the difference in exposure between the subject and the background is not extremely high. If the background in your photo is washed out to pure white, you probably won't be able to make much of a positive change. If the subject's facial features are almost impossible to pick out or in extremely deep shadow, you probably won't be able to restore them to a very flattering appearance.

Adjust Backlighting

When the foreground subject isn't too badly exposed but the background is a lot lighter than you'd like it, then the Adjust Backlighting function can often help by darkening the overexposed areas in the background.

Fill Flash

When the background is well exposed but the foreground is darker than you'd like it, Fill Flash can help by lightening these dark foreground areas.

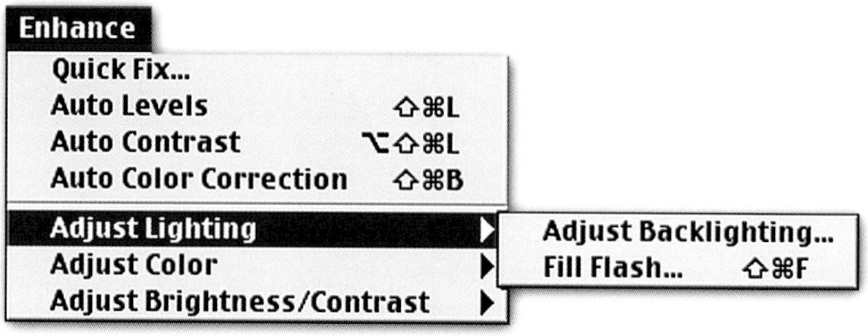

To open the Adjust Backlighting or Adjust Fill Flash dialog box, go to Enhance>Adjust Lighting and select the desired tool from the menu.

PREVIEW BOX

When you see a Preview check box in a window, be sure to leave it checked. This will allow you to instantly preview the changes you are making.

1 Open an image in Elements. In the image on the left, the subject isn't too badly exposed, but the background is too light. In the image on the right, the sunset looks nice, but the foreground area (couple, chairs, and grass) could be lighter.

2 To darken the background, go to Enhance>Adjust Lighting>Adjust Backlighting and move the Darker slider to the right until the background looks better. To lighten the foreground, select Fill Flash from the Adjust Lighting menu. Adjust the Lighter slider until the brightness on the foreground looks better. If the colors seem washed out, use the Saturation slider to correct them.

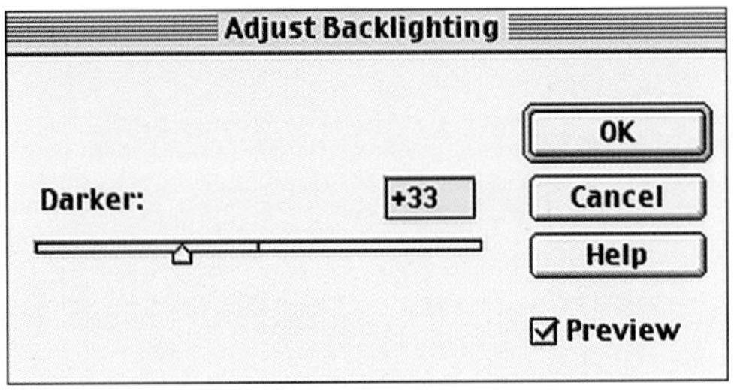

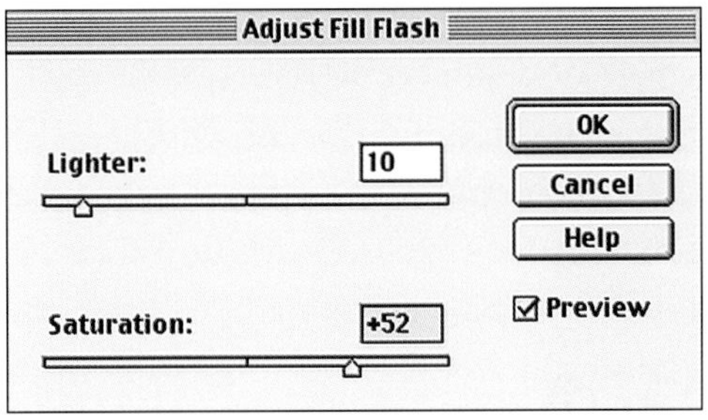

3 In the image on the left, this adjustment produced a better exposed background. In the image on the right, the foreground is better exposed. Some additional tweaking could help both photos, but they are still much better.

BRIGHTNESS/CONTRAST

One of the easiest ways to improve the overall look of your image is to increase the brightness and/or contrast slightly—but don't go overboard or the results can be really unappealing.

The *brightness* of an image refers to its overall lightness or darkness. The *contrast* of an image refers to the difference in brightness between the lightest and darkest tones in that image. Ideally, we can adjust these variables to produce an image with a full range of tones (from very dark to very light), where the subject is represented accurately (not too light or too dark).

However, the Brightness/Contrast tool can be overused. If you make an image too bright, too dark, or too contrasty, you will lose detail in some part of that image. This may be acceptable in some cases, but is usually not desirable—so adjust these settings carefully.

To adjust the brightness or contrast, go to Enhance>Adjust Brightness/Contrast>Brightness/Contrast. This will open a dialog box like the one shown to the right. Usually, you'll want to increase the contrast (move the bottom slider to the right of center). Keep an eye on the darkest and lightest areas of your image as you do so. If you adjust the contrast so that it is very high, you'll see that these areas will start to lose detail (becoming pure white or pure black). If you want to create a natural-looking image, this is something you generally want to avoid.

Use your best judgment when adjusting the brightness of the image. Depending on the subject matter, the style of the image and the look you are going for, the adjustments you make may vary widely from image to image.

Two examples (one good, one bad) of these adjustments are shown on the facing page.

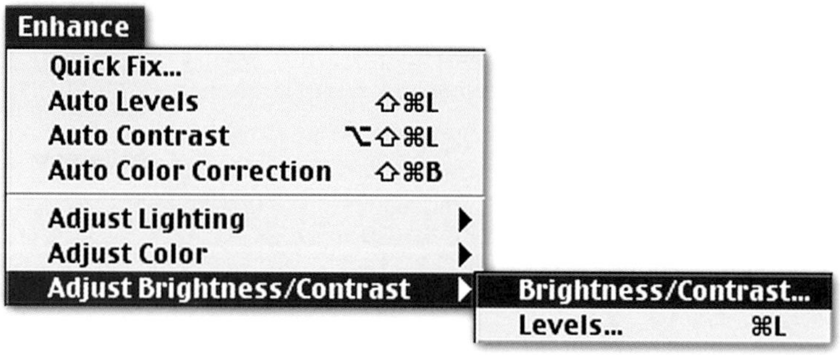

To open the Brightness/Contrast dialog box, go to Enhance>Adjust Brightness/Contrast and select the tool from the menu.

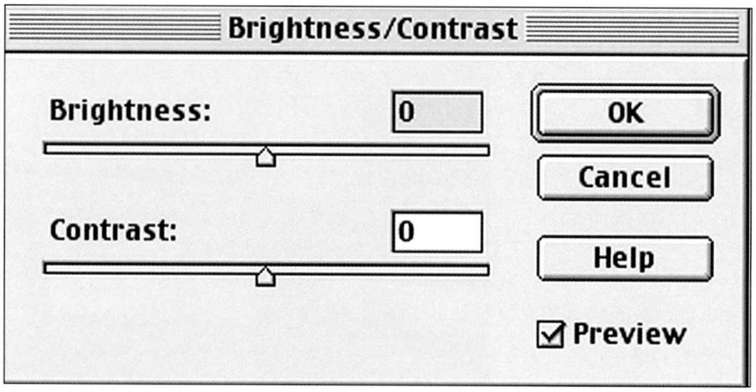

Increase the brightness of the image by moving the top slider to the right of center. Increase the contrast of the image by moving the bottom slider to the right of center.

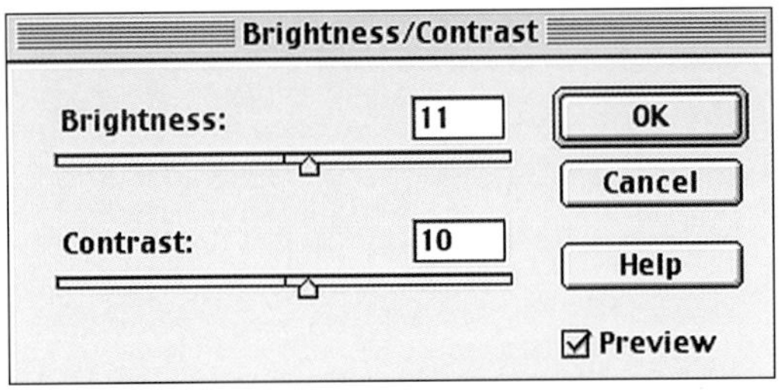

The original photo (top left) lacked contrast and was somewhat too dark. Adjustments were made in the Brightness/Contrast dialog box (above) to brighten the image and boost its contrast. The resulting image (top right) shows a big improvement!

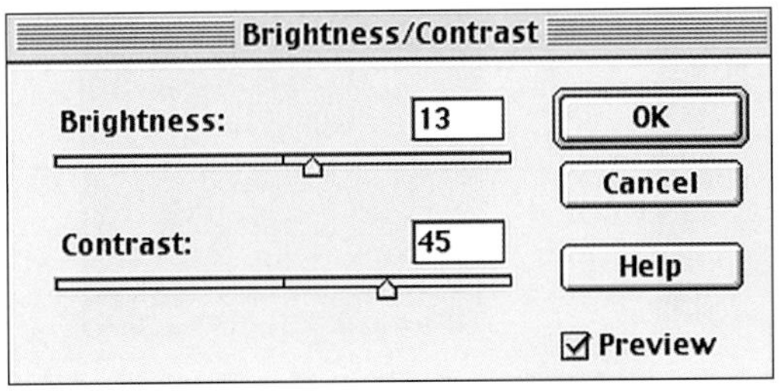

Beginning from the same original photograph as the example at the top of the page, the contrast and brightness were increased much more (above). The result (right) is just not pleasant—there is none of the detail that we'd like to see in a photo. This is especially evident in the highlights and shadows, which are pure white and black.

ADJUST COLOR

The Adjust Color menu contains some extremely useful and intuitive tools for getting your colors just right—or for changing them completely, depending on what you want to do with your image.

When you want to make quick color changes, the Enhance>Adjust Color commands are useful. They also offer some creative possibilities that will add some variety to your images.

Color Cast

When you select this tool, the box shown below appears, and your cursor turns into an eyedropper. Click on any neutral (gray, black, or white) tone in the image to remove any color cast.

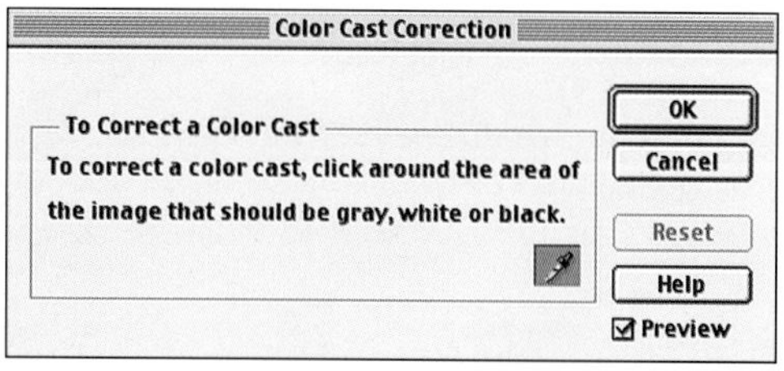

The Color Cast Correction dialog box.

Hue/Saturation

The Hue/Saturation command allows you to select a range of colors from an image (say, all the reds) and adjust them without changing the other colors. To do this, select the color you want to change from the Edit pull-down menu at the top of the dialog box. Making sure that the Preview box at the lower right is checked, adjust the Hue slider to change the color. The Saturation slider, below it, allows you to adjust the intensity of the color. The Lightness slider does just what its name suggests.

With the Colorize feature activated (at the lower right of the dialog box), the Hue/Saturation command lets you render an image in a monotone color—excellent for creating the look of a sepia-toned image. To do this, click Colorize, then drag the Hue slider to the left or right until you like the color. When using this feature, it is often desirable to slightly reduce the saturation of the new color in the image.

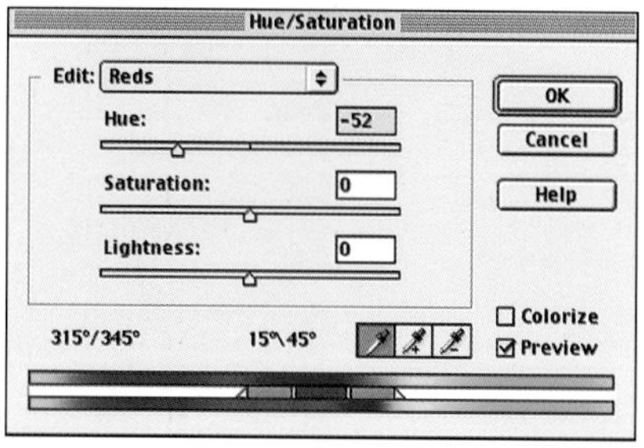

Setting the Edit pull-down menu to red and dragging the Hue slider to the left, the red window frame was changed to purple without affecting the other colors in the image.

This color image was given a sepia look using the Colorize feature in the Hue/ Saturation dialog box.

Color Variations

When you open this tool, a box appears with your "before" image in the top left and eight preview images at the bottom. Simply click on these to accept the change shown in the preview—and you can keep clicking box after box until your image looks just right (or, if you get off track, just click the Reset Image button to start over). Using the buttons at the bottom left of the box, you can make changes to primarily the highlights, midtones, shadows, or the overall saturation. With the slider under these buttons, you can adjust the settings to make big changes with each click or very subtle ones, depending on how you want or need to change your image. When the "after" image at the top right looks the way you want it, hit OK to apply the changes.

Replace Color

Replace Color works a lot like Hue/Saturation, except you pick one color in your image that you want to change by clicking on it after opening the dialog box. Under the preview of the image in the dialog box, click Selection and the areas that will be affected by your changes to the sliders at the bottom of the box will be shown in white in the image preview. The Fuzziness slider at the top of the box controls how liberal Elements will be when determining which colors in your image fall into your color range. (You can refine your color selection using the + and – eyedroppers under the Preview box and clicking on colors in the image.) Once you've selected the color(s) that you want to change, adjust the sliders as you like.

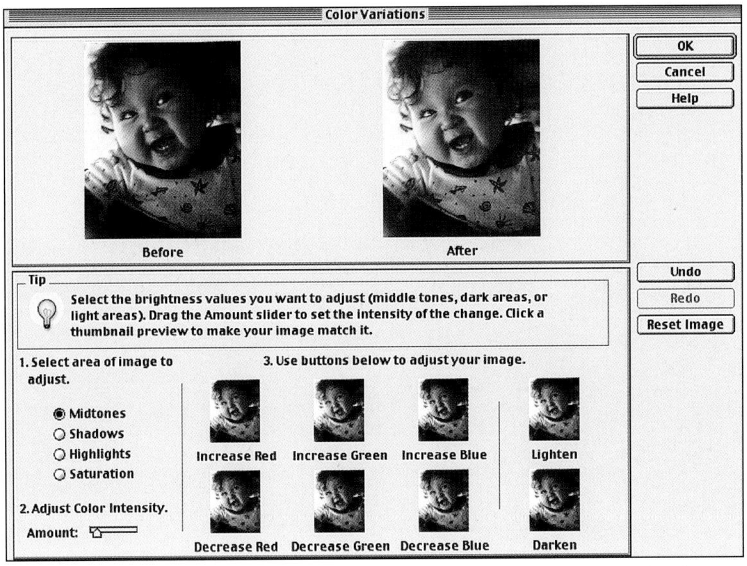

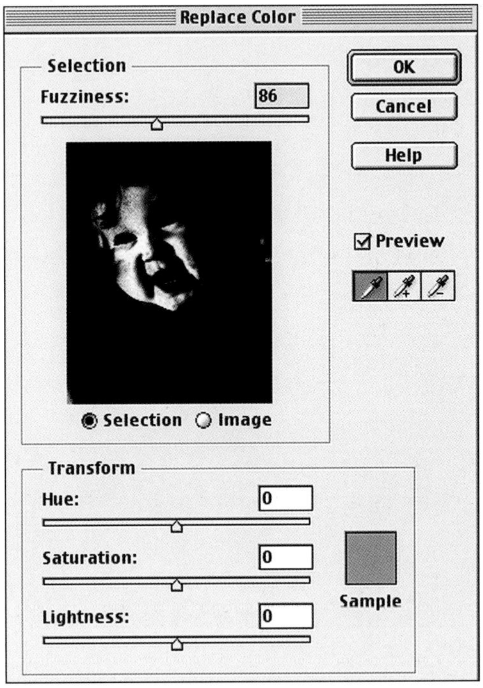

The Color Variations (above) and Replace Color (right) dialog boxes.

A FEW MORE TOOLS

Not all color correction has to make an image look the way the scene or subject actually looked when you took the picture—you can make it look better, more interesting, or even totally bizarre.

These tools affect the color and/or exposure of your image—and often in some very interesting ways. The results you'll achieve can be useful and enhance your creativity.

Equalize

When you apply the Equalize command, Elements makes the brightest tone in the image white and the darkest one black, then evenly redistributes the rest of the pixels in between. The results range from pretty good to totally awful—but it's worth a try for images where only small changes are needed. Adobe suggests using it as an initial correction to scans that look a little darker and flatter than the original image.

Gradient Map

The Gradient Map command uses a pre-existing gradient (see page 101) to map color data over the equivalent tonal range of your image. The dark tones in your image will be replaced by the color at one end of the gradient, while the light tones will be replaced by the color at the other end. The midtones will be replaced by the gradations in between. To apply the effect, select a gradient from the pull-down menu in the Gradient Map dialog box (the default setting is a gradient from the current

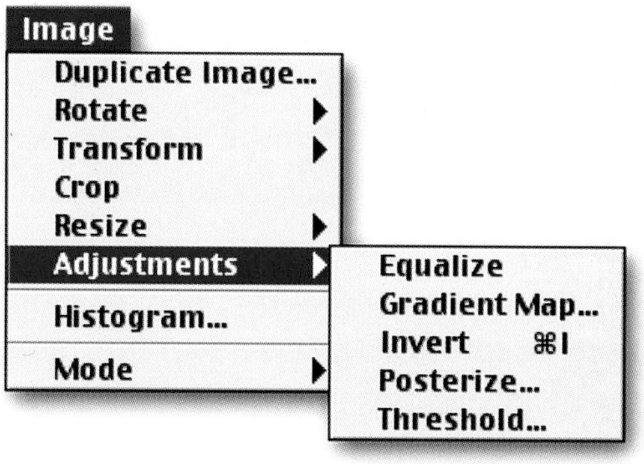

To try these effects, go to Image>Adjustments and select the desired options from the pull-down menu.

The turtle shown above underwent some drastic color changes thanks to the Gradient Map command.

The image in the center is a color photograph with a strong graphic quality (meaning it's the shapes in the photo more than the textures that make it interesting). Inverted (left), the image becomes very different—almost ghostly. Posterizing the image (right) to four levels makes the image even more graphic—with almost no fine detail.

foreground color to the current background color), and watch what happens.

Invert

The Invert command evaluates the tones and colors in an image and then switches them to their opposites—blues become yellow, blacks become white, etc. The resulting image is essentially a negative of the original. On black & white originals, the results are pretty predictable; with color images, the results can be a bit more surprising.

Posterize

Posterization reduces the range of tones in an image to a limited number. The resulting images have very little detail. When you access the Posterize command, a dialog box will appear. In this box, the single control option is the number of levels. Setting this at 2 will produce an image that is made up of only of two colors. With higher settings, more tones will be used.

Threshold

The Threshold command converts your image into a very high-contrast black & white photo. When you select this, a dialog box appears to help you adjust the effect. By adjusting the slider to the left or right you can control which tones are black and which are white. To learn how to read histograms (the jagged stuff above the slider) see pages 58–59.

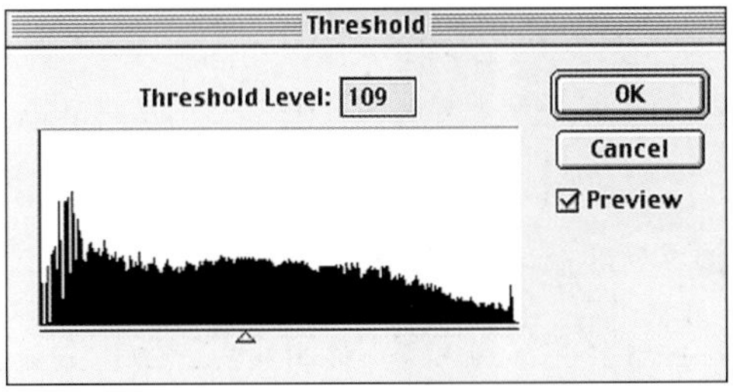

The Threshold dialog box.

CHAPTER SIX

Levels and the Eyedropper Tool

The automated tools covered in the previous chapter are very useful in many situations, but sometimes they just don't provide the degree of control needed. Using the Levels and Eyedropper tools in partnership will give you more precise control for enhanced results.

EVALUATING IMAGES

When you want to make the most of an image, you can't just start hitting buttons and hope everything will work out; you need a concise plan of action.

As with any endeavor, developing a plan of action before diving in will enhance your success. When you scan or open an image and notice that it needs to be color corrected (or if you open it because it needs color help), you'll need to figure out exactly what the problem is. The following are some of the things you should look for when trying to decide what to do.

Shadows and Highlights

One thing that can make any photo look less than perfect is the absence of at least some areas of deep black and bright white. For most images, achieving a pleasing look requires the use of the full range of tones from black to white. Our eyes adjust to see this full range of colors in the world around us, so if a photo lacks it we immediately feel that the image looks flat or dull.

Ask yourself: Are the darkest areas in your photo dark enough? Are the lightest areas light enough? Some photos may have one problem, some may have both, and some may have no problem at all. If you are looking at a scanned image, keep in mind that scanning can negatively affect the image, so even if your original was good, you may still need to adjust the scan.

There are, or course, some exceptions. If you've taken a photograph of a marshmallow in a snow bank, there may well not be any deep, dark tones. In an image of a black cat in a coal bin, there may not be any areas of pure white. Such instance are very rare, however. There may also be instances where, for creative reasons, you choose not to use the full range of tones in your image. In that case, you can move on to the next category of analysis.

Neutrals

Neutral tones (areas of white or gray) are often the key to learning what's going on under the skin of a digital image. If the neutral tones have a color cast, chances are that the rest of the image does too.

A good place to start is with the whites. Keep in mind, the whites you evaluate should be areas of pure (or very close to pure) white—like a cloud, a white piece of clothing, etc. Although we often refer to the "whites" of the eyes or to people's teeth being white, they rarely are. Once you've identified an area to evaluate, examine it closely for any slight shifts in color—white that looks at first glance to be pure often turns out on closer inspection to be faintly yellow, or blue, or pink. A small color cast may be fine—this is a subjective decision that is yours to make. For example, if white clouds on a blue sky have a slight bluish cast, that may not be objectionable. (But if that bluish cast runs through your whole image and makes your portrait subject look blue, that could be a big problem indeed.)

Grays should also be neutral in tone (not bluish gray or reddish gray). Here, the selection of an area to evaluate is much more subjective. Paved streets (in most areas) tend to be a reasonably neutral gray. Sometimes clothes and other fabrics are neutral gray (and this can be either light or dark). Shadows on white walls or backdrops are also fairly neutral gray areas.

Photograph by Barbara Rice.

Skin Tones

As humans, we are accustomed to seeing human skin tones all around us every day of our lives. Therefore, we all notice it pretty quickly when a skin tone just plain doesn't look right. We notice problems especially quickly in photos of people we know personally or see on a regular basis. Yet, from time to time, we all see images of people who unintentionally look jaundiced, or seasick, or like they've spent too much time in the sun.

There are a few reasons for this. First, skin tones vary widely from person to person, and can change dramatically depending on the lighting, activity level, exposure to sun, and even the person's emotional state. Second, skin tones are also finely detailed and feature hundreds of shades of color rather than a few unified tones. Third, even subtle problems can be very obvious to viewers. While you can get away with the grass being a little off color, it's harder for viewers to overlook skin tones that miss the mark.

Because evaluating skin tones is a fairly detailed process, we'll examine it more closely on pages 68–69.

In most images, showing a full range of tones—from rich black to bright white—creates the most pleasing appearance. To evaluate this image, let's look at the blacks on the shoes. These dark areas have a strong black. The highlights (like the white threads at the bottom of the girl's jeans) also look fine. The gray boulder the family is sitting on doesn't seem to have a color cast (it looks neutral), and the skin tones seem very nice. Overall, this image passes the test. Compare this with the photo on page 68 or the photos on page 66—all of which exhibit color or exposure problems.

DIGITAL COLOR

We often take color for granted—until we start doing digital imaging. Digital imagers have a great palette of color to manipulate, and knowing how it's organized is critical for using it effectively.

If you ever took an art class (or even played around with watercolors as a kid), you probably know that combining two or more colors creates new colors. For example, combining blue paint and yellow paint makes green paint. In fact, almost all colors are actually combinations of some other colors.

Color Mode

The very few colors you can't create by combining others are called the primary colors. In digital imaging, this set of primary colors is also referred to as the image mode or color mode.

Primary Colors

There are two sets of primary colors, but Elements only supports one: the subtractive primary colors. This is the set of primaries used to create color by devices that produce light—like monitors, digital camera LCD screens, and television screens. (The other set of primary colors, called additive, is used in situations where color is created by light being reflected off another surface—like the page of a book.)

The subtractive primary colors are red, green, and blue. Thus, the corresponding color mode is called RGB. These colors are called subtractive because the total absence of all of the colors in an area is what produces black. If you remember that these colors are produced as light, this makes a lot of sense—after all, the total absence of light creates total darkness (black). At the other extreme, the full-strength presence of all of the colors produces white. You can see this in the center of

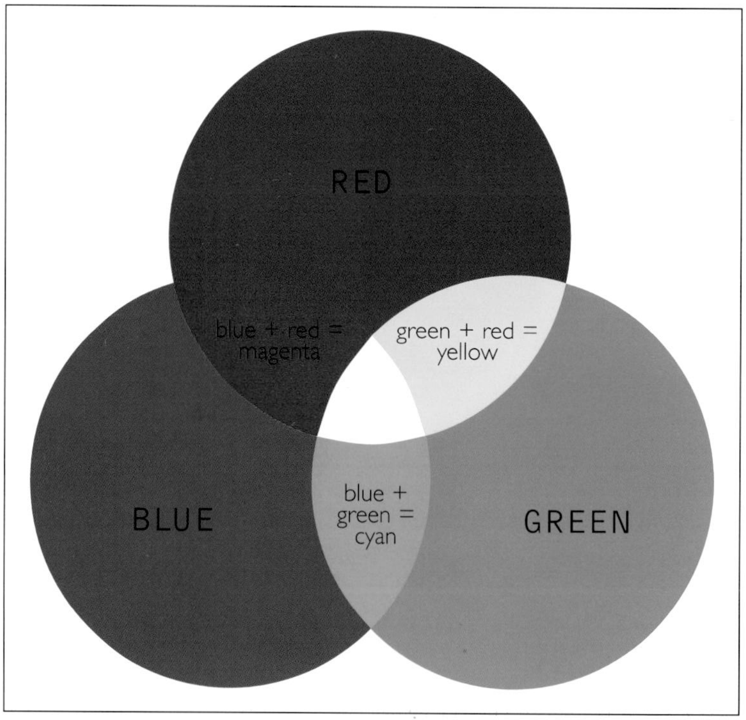

As you can see by looking at the center of the grouping, the presence of all colors yields white when using the RGB set of primary colors. When red and green are combined in equal amounts, the result is yellow. Combining blue and green in equal amounts produces cyan (bluish green). Combining blue and red in equal amounts produces magenta.

the diagram on the facing page, which shows the effect of combining any two colors (at the overlaps between primary colors) and all three colors (center).

Color Recipes

The amount of a primary color that is present in a given non-primary color is noted as a value that ranges from 0 (not there at all) to 255 (present at its fullest strength). This means that, in the digital world, we can identify individual colors using a pretty precise "recipe," which is extremely helpful when we want to make sure that the colors in a sequence of images match, for instance.

Color recipes are usually written something like this: R50/G120/B201. Looking at a recipe like this tells us that the red (R) value is 50, the green (G) value is 120, and the blue (B) value is 201. As you become more familiar with digital imaging, you'll be able to figure out what a color looks like just by reading the recipe. For now, here are a few things to keep in mind. First, if all the values are 256, the color is white. If they are all 0, the color is black. If the colors are all the same value (but not 0 or 256), the color is a shade of gray. Also, the bigger the number, the stronger the presence of that color in the image. If all the numbers are high, the color will be quite light; if all are low, the color will be quite dark. Some examples are shown below to help you get a feel for this.

We'll be working with this throughout the chapter, so don't be intimidated if it seems daunting—it will become more clear as you put it into practice!

R0/G0/B0 | R102/G102/B102 | R178/G178/B178 | R255/G255/B255

The R, G, and B values are equal in each color swatch. As the values get higher, the color goes from black, to shades of gray, to white.

R0/G0/B255 | R0/G0/B175 | R0/G0/B100 | R0/G0/B50

Only blue (B) is used. As the numbers get smaller, the blue gets darker.

R100/G100/B50 | R100/G100/B100 | R100/G100/B150 | R100/G100/B200

The R and G values are constant. As the blue changes, the color shifts from green (weak blue), to gray (blue equal to red and green), to shades of blue (strong blue).

EYEDROPPER TOOL

As mentioned previously, your eyes will deceive you. Fortunately, the Eyedropper tool will not. Therefore, it can work as your "lie detector" when you want to make precise color decisions.

Once you've opened your image in Elements, you have two tools for evaluating it: your eyes and the Eyedropper tool. Your eyes provide subjective results; the Eyedropper tool, located near the bottom of the Tool bar (see page 13), provides results that are totally objective.

On pages 38–39, we examined how the eye—or actually, the brain—treats color subjectively and can sometimes fool us into thinking things look different than they actually do. This makes the objectivity of the Eyedropper tool especially valuable when you are trying to closely analyze colors.

The Eyedropper tool samples colors, allowing you to see the precise color value of pixels (displayed in the Info palette) as you evaluate an image. This information is expressed in terms of the RGB values that make up the colors, as discussed on pages 52–53.

When you move the Eyedropper over a very dark area of your image, you'll see that the Info palette shows low RGB values. As you'll recall from pages 52–53, this is because RGB is a subtractive color model, meaning that the absence of all of the colors yields black—so the lower the RGB values, the darker the color.

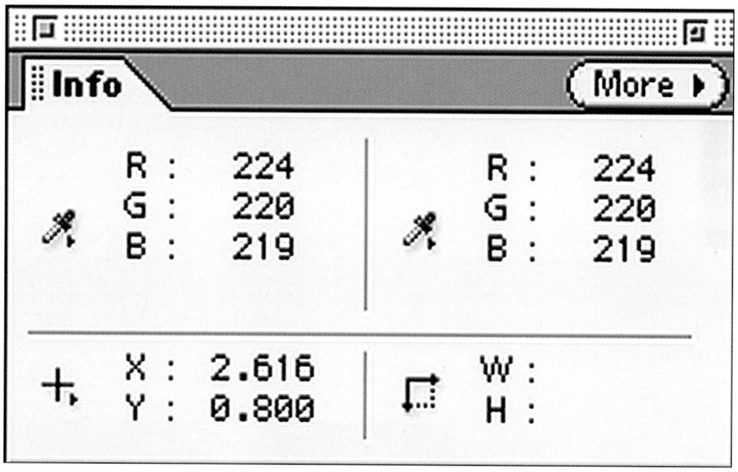

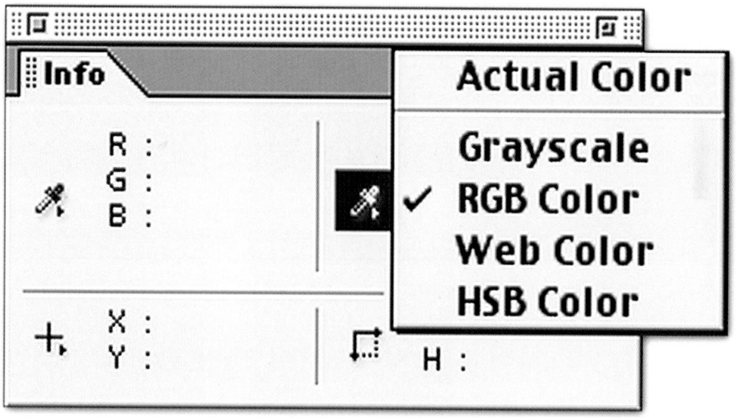

The Info palette (top) shows you the data gathered by the Eyedropper tool. If the top left or right half reads anything other than RGB, click on the eyedropper icon in the box and select RGB Color from the drop-down menu (above). This is the mode we'll work in throughout this book.

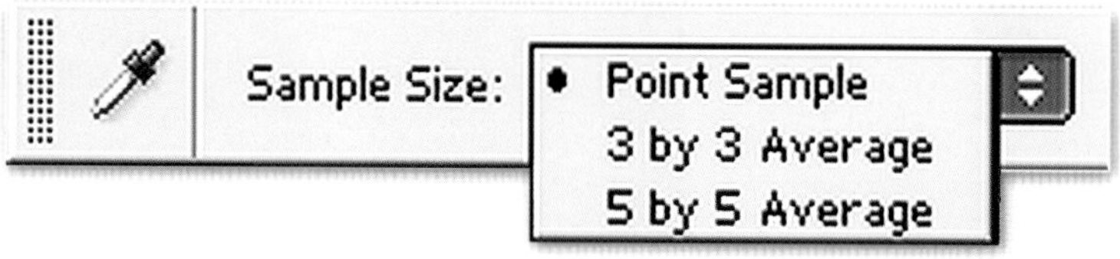

From the Options bar for the Eyedropper tool, select 3 by 3 Average.

1 Open a color image in Elements and select the Eyedropper tool.

2 In the Options bar at the top of the screen, set the sample area to 3 by 3 Average. This allows you to read the average value of three pixels within the area you click on in the next step. This averaged reading provides a better sense of the tone and color of the area than reading a single pixel.

3 Next, verify that the Info palette is visible on your screen. If it's not, go to Window>Info.

4 With the Eyedropper tool still active, move your cursor over your image and watch the Info palette. You'll notice that the RGB values change as you move the cursor over different areas of the frame. Move the cursor to dark areas, light areas, and areas of different colors.

Photograph by Barbara Rice.

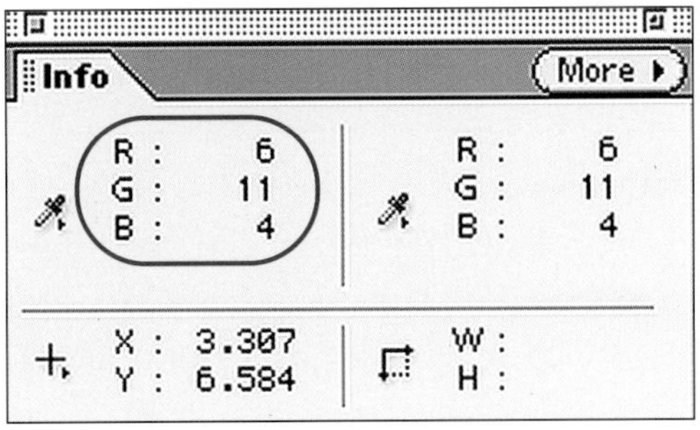

Sample 1—The values in the shadow area on the horse are all very low. This tells us that the area is almost black.

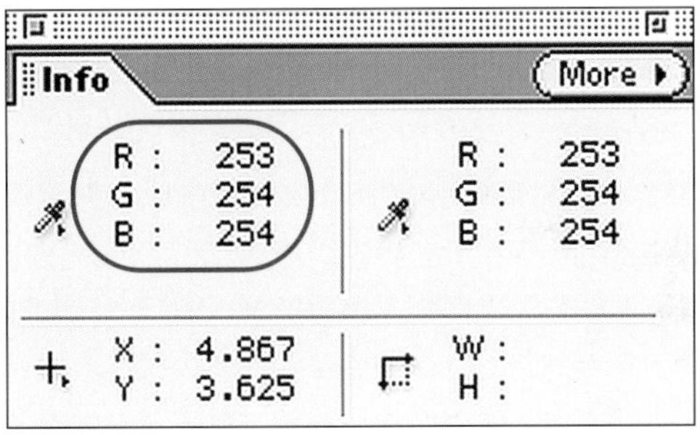

Sample 2—The values in the highlight area on the horse's nose are all very high. This tells us that the area is almost white.

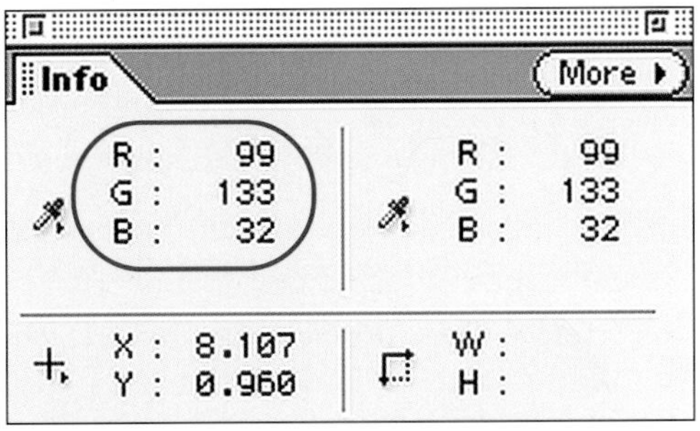

Sample 3—When the green leaves are sampled, the G value is high. The R value is also quite high, indicating this is a yellowish green (remember, green plus red equals yellow—see page 52.)

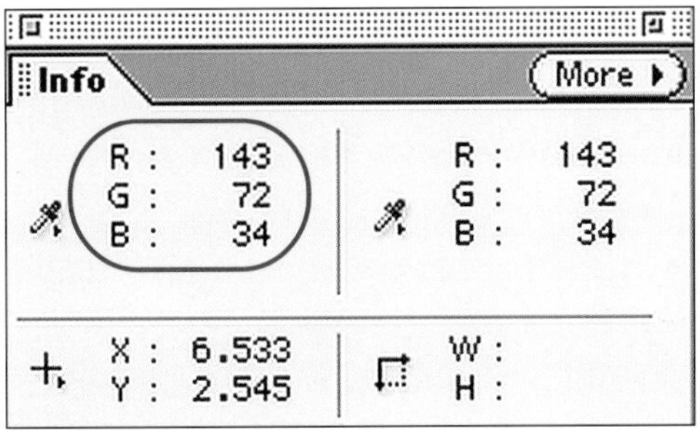

Sample 4—When a red leaf is sampled, the R value is high. The G value is also a bit high (compared to the B value), indicating that this leaf is an orangish red.

LEVELS—THE BASICS

The Levels are a slightly more complicated way of adjusting the tones in your image, but they also offer the greater degree of control you need to make very fine adjustments.

The color- and exposure-correction tools we've looked at so far offer quick solutions to some problems, but they don't provide much precision. With the auto commands (Auto Contrast, etc.), you either like the results or you don't—there's no way to fine-tune them. With functions like Brightness/ Contrast, your adjustments change all the tones equally. So what if you want to darken the shadows without changing the rest of the image? What if you want to brighten the midtones (all of the areas of middle brightness that are neither shadow nor highlight) without impacting the shadows or the highlights?

To accomplish these tasks and take control of the colors and tones in your image, you need to master Levels, which lets you make changes to just the midtones without affecting the shadows, or just the highlights without impacting the midtones, etc. The result is a much greater degree of control.

The Dialog Box

The following is an overview of the features of the Levels dialog box. Don't worry if the individual elements seem a little abstract—on the next few pages we'll look at some practical examples that will make everything clear.

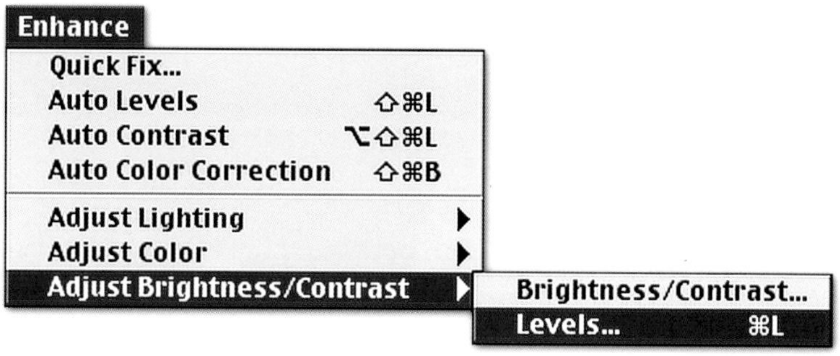

To access the Levels, open an image and then go to Enhance>Adjust Brightness/Contrast> Levels.

When you open the Levels dialog box, the first thing you'll probably notice is a jagged black shape in a white window (1, facing page). This is called a histogram, and it is a graphic representation of the tonal values in your individual image. This histogram is one of the most valuable features of the Levels tool, since it gives you a totally objective way to evaluate your image.

Under the histogram are three triangular sliders. At the left is the black shadow slider (2), under the area of the histogram that shows dark tones. In the center is the gray midtone slider (3), under the area of the histogram that shows the midtones. On the right is the white highlight slider (4), under the highlight area of the histogram. The taller the histogram is above each area, the more of the tones in the image fall into that tonal range. By clicking and dragging these sliders, you can change the tonal range and contrast of your

The Levels dialog box has many features.

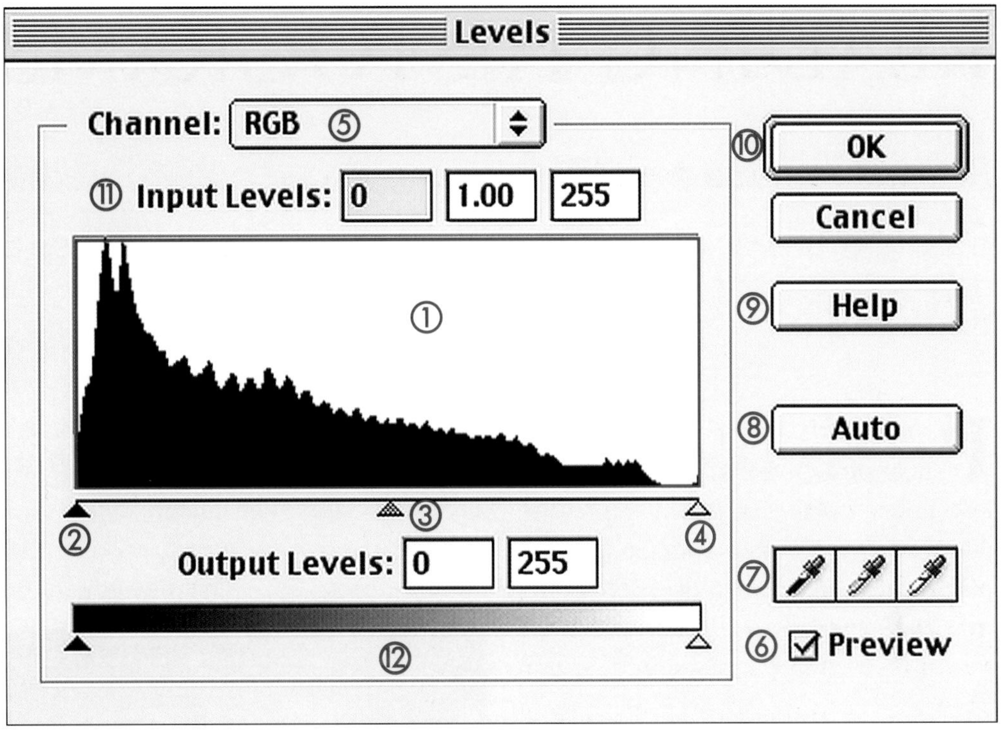

image (see page 60–63 for further details on this process).

At the top of the box is the Channel menu (5). There is one channel for each primary color in your image—red, green, and blue—as well as a composite channel for all three together (RGB). As we'll see on pages 64–65, this gives you some powerful ways to adjust colors.

When using Levels, make sure that the Preview box (6) is checked so that you can see the results of your changes.

At the bottom right are three eyedroppers (7). From left to right, these are the Set Black Point eyedropper, the Set Gray Point eyedropper, and the Set White Point eyedropper. These will be covered in detail on pages 66–67.

Clicking the Auto button (8) does the same thing as hitting Enhance>Auto Levels. See page 41 for more on this.

The Help button (9) takes you to the Elements help file for Levels, while the OK and Cancel buttons (10) are used to accept or decline any changes made in the dialog box.

The Input Levels (11) show numerically the full range of tones in the image. Each box corresponds to one of the sliders under the histogram. In the RGB color mode, the left box will read 0 (zero) for pure black and corresponds to the black slider. The box on the right will read 255 for pure white and corresponds to the white slider. The middle slider corresponds to the midtone slider and will be set to 1.0. If you move the sliders, you will notice that the values change in the Input Levels boxes.

The Output Levels (12) allow you to control the extent of the tonal range in the final image, normally to ensure that it does not exceed the capabilities of an output device. This is not an important feature for most people—unless you are printing images on a printing press.

READING HISTOGRAMS

Reading the histogram for your image can tell you quite a lot about it. Even if you didn't know what the image looked like, you could get a pretty good idea about its basic characteristics.

Probably the most useful component of the Levels dialog box is the histogram. Using this graphic representation of the tones in your image, it's easy to get a good idea of where there might be problems. Let's look at a couple of examples using the Levels to evaluate an image. The images below are each paired with a screen shot of the Levels dialog box. The histogram for

These images are each paired with a screen shot of their Levels dialog box. As you can see, the histograms are very different.

Photographs by Jeff Smith.

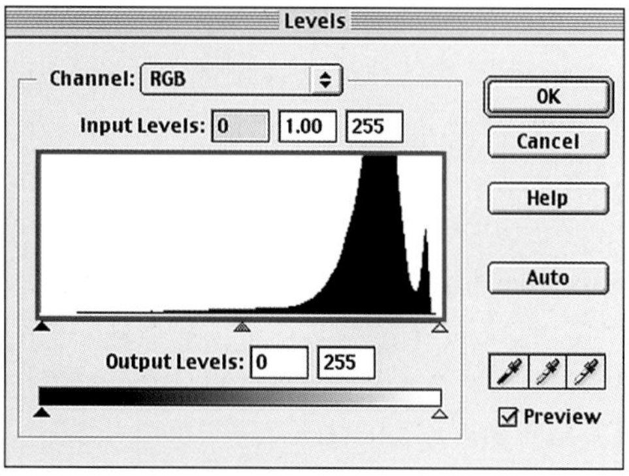

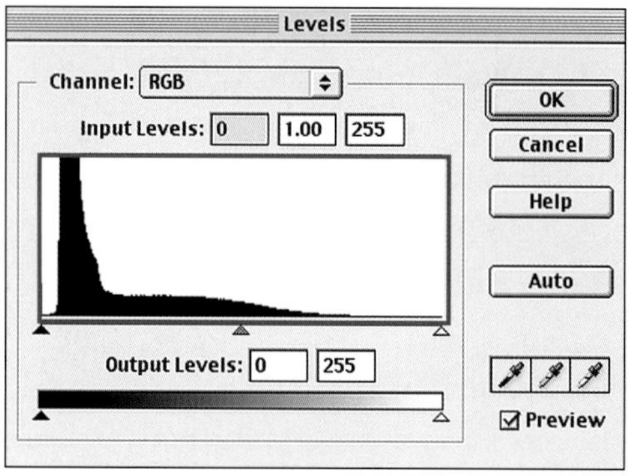

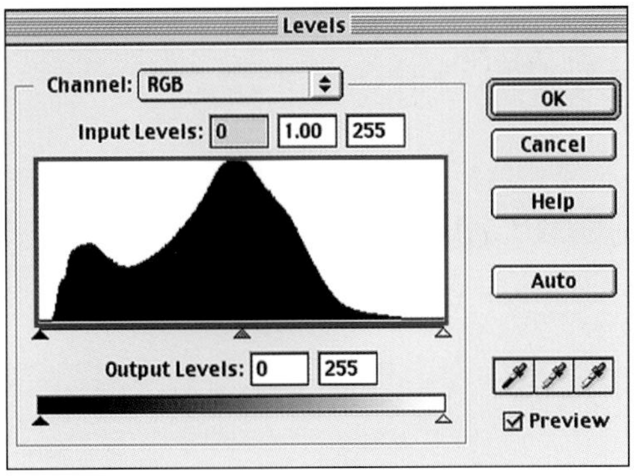

In most images, you'll see that the data is more evenly distributed across the entire range of the histogram. Compare this image and histogram with the ones on the facing page.

Photograph by Jeff Smith.

each is boxed in red. As you can see, the histograms are very different.

If you look at the portrait of the young woman (facing page), you'll notice that the tones in the image are almost all white or very light. Now, look at the screen shot below that image. In this example, the histogram is very tall near the highlight end of the histogram. That tells us that most of the tones in this image are pretty bright. Notice the height of the histogram over the midtone slider—pretty low. This tells us that very few of the tones in the image fall into this category. Now, look at the histogram above the black slider. As you can see, there's nothing there; none of the tones in this image are pure black. From evaluating the histogram, you can therefore see one quality of this image that might need attention.

If you look at the image of the young man, you'll see that quite the opposite is true. The histogram in the region of the black slider is very high, and quite a few tones also fall into the midtone category. Looking at the histogram over the white slider, you can see that very little of the image (see the bright stars in the background) displays this level of brightness. Even if you did not have the image to look at, you could tell just by looking at the histograms that this is an image with predominantly very dark tones, that some tones are a bit lighter, and that a very small amount of the image is made up of very light tones.

In most images, you'll see that the data is more evenly distributed across the entire range of the histogram, as seen in the photo above and the screen shot to the left of it.

DIGITAL CAMERAS

Elements isn't the only place you'll find histograms—many digital cameras also allow you to display them for each image. Look for this under your camera's image-review settings. Learning to read histograms can, therefore, be an asset both when creating and editing images.

ADJUSTING CONTRAST

Here's where histograms start to get really useful, giving you an indicator of potential problems with images—subtle things you might not notice at first glance but that can improve your photos.

Now that you know the basics of reading a histogram, let's look at how these histograms can help you diagnose image problems—and how adjusting the sliders can help you correct them. In this lesson, we'll look at contrast.

The overall tonal range and contrast of an image is sometimes easier to evaluate objectively using the Levels histogram. In the example to the right, the low contrast of the photograph is obvious in the histogram, which shows that the tonal range of the image does not extend as much as it could into either the black or the white range. Unless this is intentional, you'd probably want to consider strategies for improving the contrast of such an image.

The quickest way to do this is to move the highlight and shadow sliders. Begin by moving the shadow slider to the right until it is just under the edge of the histogram data (you can ignore any flat little tail of data that might stick out here, as seen in the screen shot to the right). When you do this, you're telling Elements that the darkest tone in your image (represented by that far left end of the histogram) should actually be black. Similarly, moving the highlight slider to the left until it is just under the

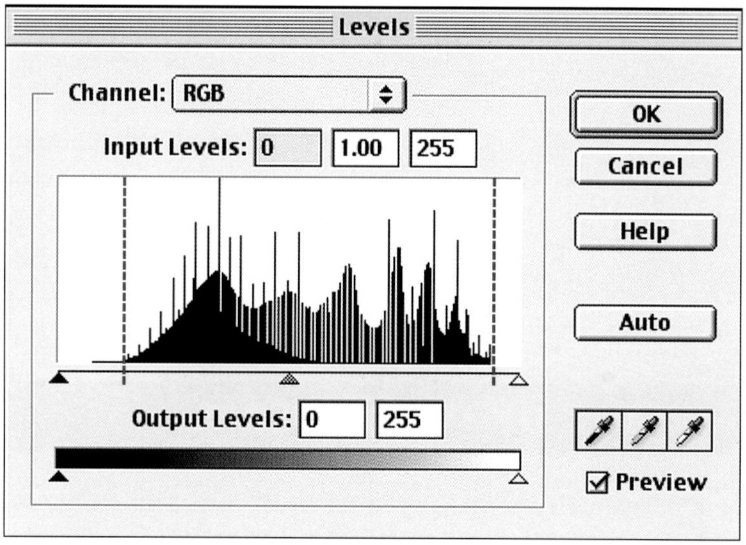

Notice how the histogram data stops short of the shadow and highlight sliders. This reveals that the tones in this image do not extend through the full tonal range from black to white. As a result, the image looks flat and muddy; it suffers from a lack of contrast.

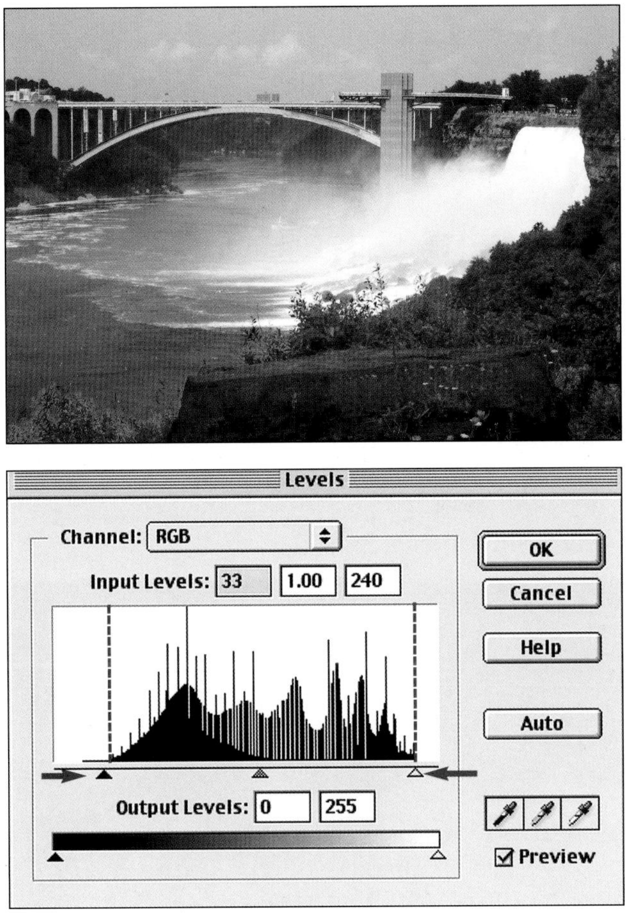

Clicking and dragging the shadow and highlight sliders in under the very edge of the histogram data above them fixes the contrast. The tones in this image (reflected by the histogram) now extend all the way from black to white.

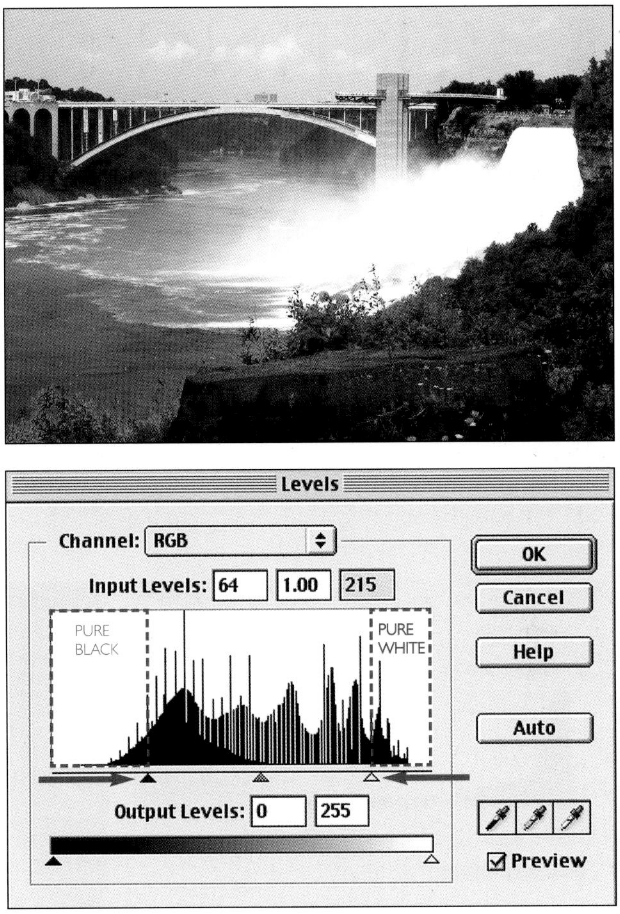

Don't move the highlight or shadow slider in past the edge of the histogram—this will destroy the detail in your image. All the tones to the left of the shadow slider will be pure black; all the tones to the right of the highlight slider will be pure white.

edge of the histogram data tells Elements that you want the lightest tone in your image to be white. This operation is shown in the image and screen shot on the left (above).

If moving the highlight and shadow sliders in a little is *good*, moving them in a lot must be *better*, right? Nope. In the photograph and screen shot on the right (above), you can see what happens when you do this. When the shadow slider is moved in too far under the histogram, all of the image tones to the left of it in the histogram become pure black with no subtle detail. Similarly, all of the tones in the histogram that fall to the right of the highlight slider become pure white with no detail.

For the majority of photos, ones where a realistic look is desired, this results in contrast that is too high. The areas of undetailed white and black can look especially ugly when printed, since this tends to make the problem even more evident than it is on-screen.

If you want a creative effect that doesn't need to be realistic, however, you might actually *want* to use this method to create an image with extremely high contrast.

ADJUSTING THE MIDTONES

If the highlights and shadows look good in your image but something still doesn't look quite right with the exposure, the problem is likely the midtones. Try brightening or darkening them to fix the problem.

For many photos, a simple adjustment to the midtones can make a big improvement. This is very easy to do in the Levels dialog box.

To brighten the midtones in an image, click on the midtone slider and drag it toward the black point slider. This may seem somewhat counterintu-

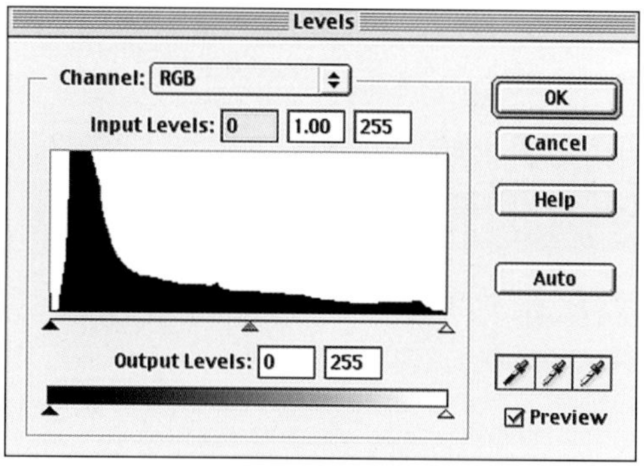

Here, the tones in the image are predominantly dark. This is just fine, but the skin tones and brightly colored t-shirts seem like they could be a bit brighter. Also, the subjects' dark hair doesn't stand out from the background very well.

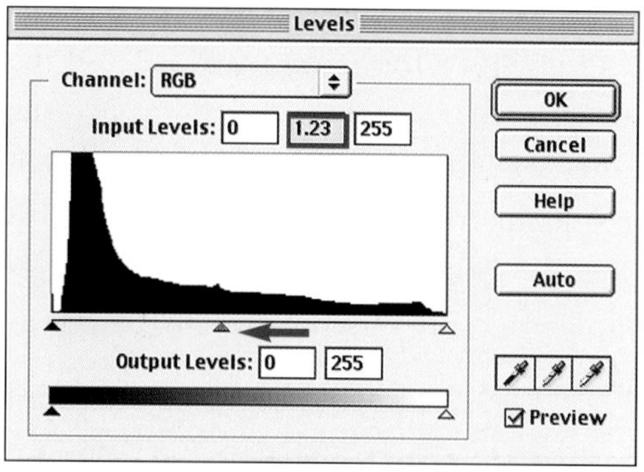

Moving the midtone slider slightly to the left makes the subjects stand out better from the background and gives a better representation of the colors. Don't go overboard with a change like this—the results can be quite unpleasant.

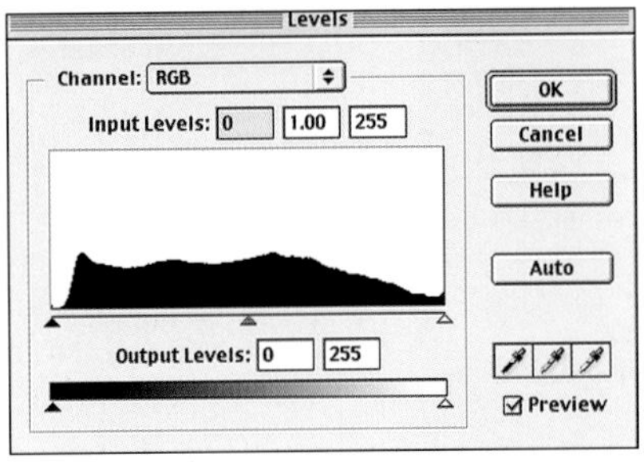

In this image, the tones are spread evenly across the histogram, but the skin tones look pretty pasty. They could be darker.

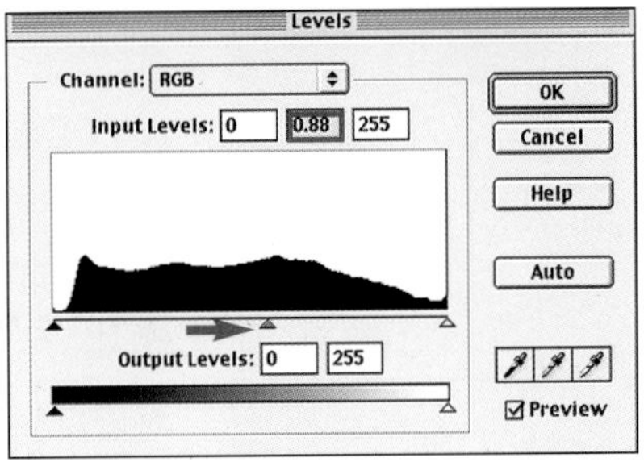

Moving the midtone slider a bit to the right darkened the midtones, making the skin tones look more healthy.

itive—wouldn't you want to drag it toward the highlight to brighten the image? Nope. Remember, the slider you are moving defines the midtone point. When you move it toward the shadow slider, that shifts the tones in the image so that more of them are *lighter* than the midtone (i.e., more of the histogram lays between the midtone slider and the white point slider than between the midtone slider and the black point slider). To darken the midtones in an image, simply move the midtone slider toward the white point slider.

A COMBINED APPROACH

The results you achieve using the auto color-correction functions can often be fine-tuned to great effect using the Levels command—especially when the results with the automatic tools are already close to what you want.

ADJUSTING THE CHANNELS

Here's where we get to the really powerful aspect of the Levels—the ability to deal with each primary color individually instead of collectively. This gives you greater control than any other tool in Elements.

As discussed on pages 52–53, the set of primary colors used to create the other colors in your image is collectively referred to as the color model or color mode. The individual colors within the set, on the other hand, are called channels. For example, if your image is in the RGB mode, then it has three channels—red, green, and blue.

Viewing the Channels

As noted on page 57, the Channels pull-down menu at the top of the Levels dialog box allows you to work on the

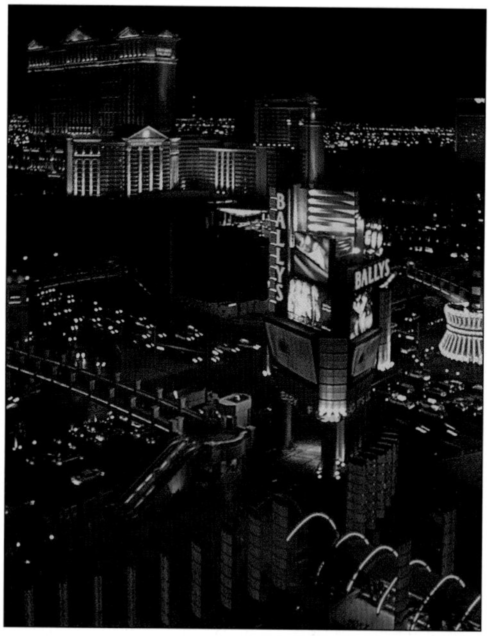

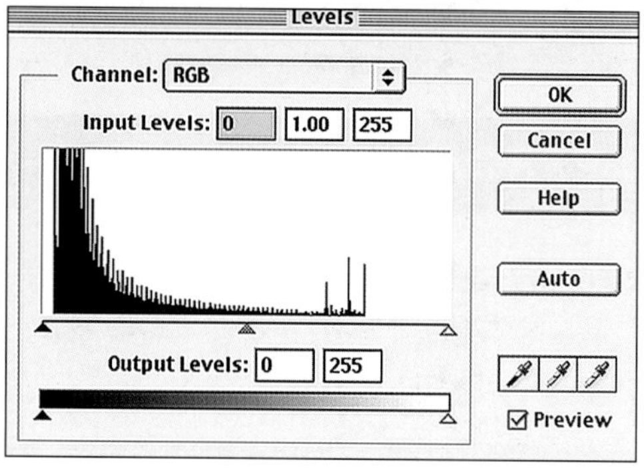

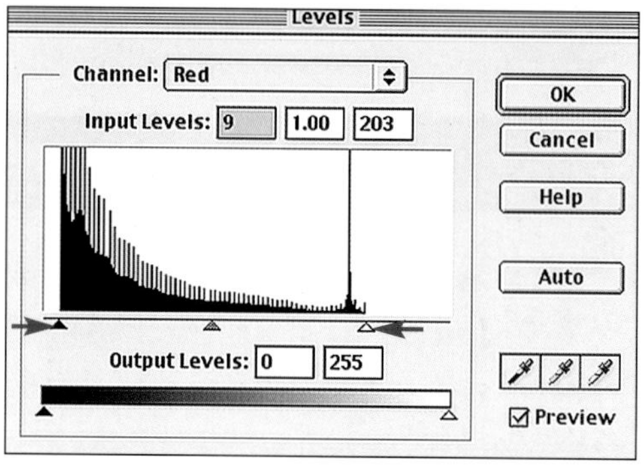

1 Open an image in the RGB color mode (far left, top). Then, go to Enhance>Adjust Brightness/Contrast>Levels to open the Levels dialog box (far left, bottom).

2 Pull down on the Channel menu at the top of the box and select the red channel. Move the highlight slider to the left until it is just under the edge of the data in the histogram. Then, move the shadow slider to the right until it is just under the edge of the image data in the histogram (bottom left).

3 Repeat this process for the green channel (right image and screen shot).

4 Repeat this process for the blue channel (far-right image and screen shot).

5 As you make each change, don't worry if the colors seem to shift in unpleasant ways; you can only see the final effect when you've completed the last change on the last channel.

6 If you want to fine-tune the results, go back into the individual channels or the composite RGB channel and try adjusting the midtone sliders.

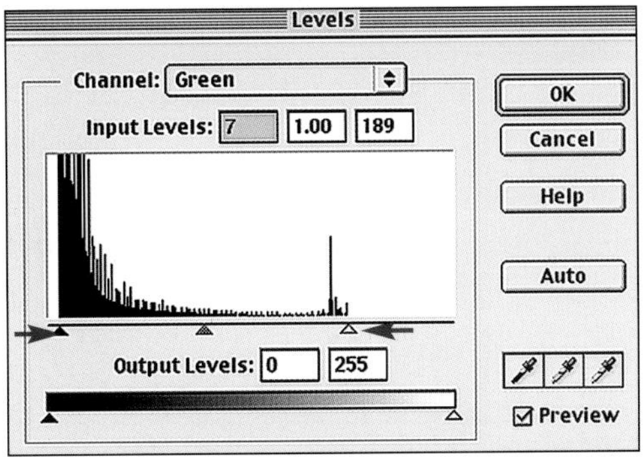

image as a whole (the RGB channel) or on individual channels one at a time.

Adjusting the Channels

By adjusting the individual channels, you can quickly remove a color cast while improving the overall contrast of your photograph. The basic procedure is easy to accomplish and can be adjusted visually to suit the individual image. Just follow the steps that begin on the facing page.

Keep in mind that you'll be able to see the changes most clearly if you work with an image that doesn't look perfect already. Here, the left image on the facing page lacks contrast and has an overall pinkish color cast. This makes it a good candidate for this technique.

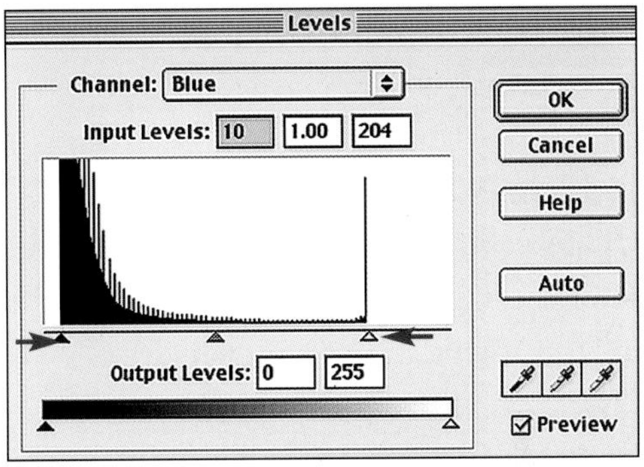

Fine-Tuning the Results

When you have completed this process, your image (in most cases) should be better color balanced and have better contrast. Evaluate your image carefully, however, to ensure that the highlights are not blown out (lacking detail) and the shadows are not blocked up (lacking detail)—unless you want the image to look that way. If the color in your images doesn't look right, you may also want to make adjustments to the midtone sliders in one or more of the individual color channels.

THE LEVELS EYEDROPPERS

Want a quick one-touch correction? The eyedroppers may be just what you're looking for. With a little experimentation, these handy little tools can produce surprisingly good results.

The eyedroppers provide a quick way to remove color casts and set the overall tonal range of your image. To use them, open an image and go to Enhance>Adjust Brightness/Contrast> Levels. You can use one, two, or all three of the eyedroppers, depending on your needs.

Set Black Point

To use the Set Black Point eyedropper, simply click on its icon at the lower right of the dialog box (see page 57). Your cursor will then turn into an eyedropper. Move the eyedropper over the image and click on an area of the image that you want to become pure black. Assuming you have the Preview box checked (at the lower-right corner of the dialog box), the image will adjust instantly to reflect the change. Don't worry if it doesn't look right—you can click again and again until you get it right. Be careful with this tool; you can easily create ugly, blocked-up areas of black with no detail.

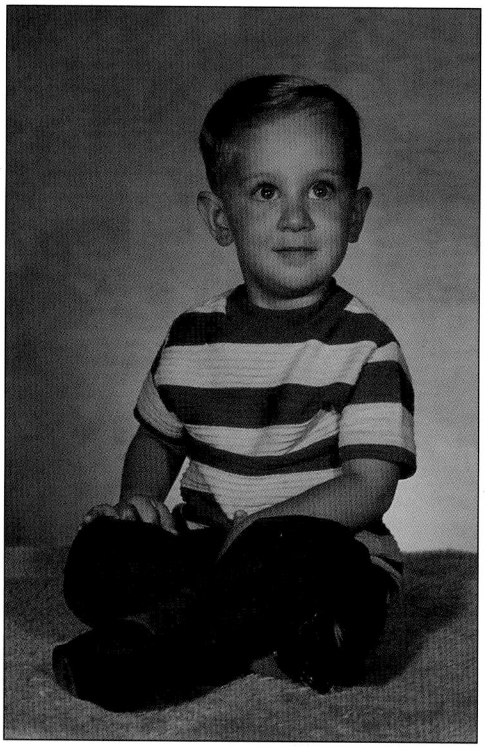

1 Photos often lose contrast and shift color over the years. The image on the far left mostly lacks contrast, but some color help won't hurt it.

2 To begin, the Set Black Point eyedropper was selected and clicked on a very dark shadow area of the little boy's shoe. This set that area to black. It also caused some of the other tones to shift (left)—but we'll fix that in the next step.

3 The Set White Point eyedropper was then clicked on a bright highlight next to the boy's left elbow (right). Alternately, you could click on one of the highlights in his eyes.

4 Since the pants should be neutral gray, the Set Gray Point eyedropper was clicked on them. This eliminated the pink color cast (far right).

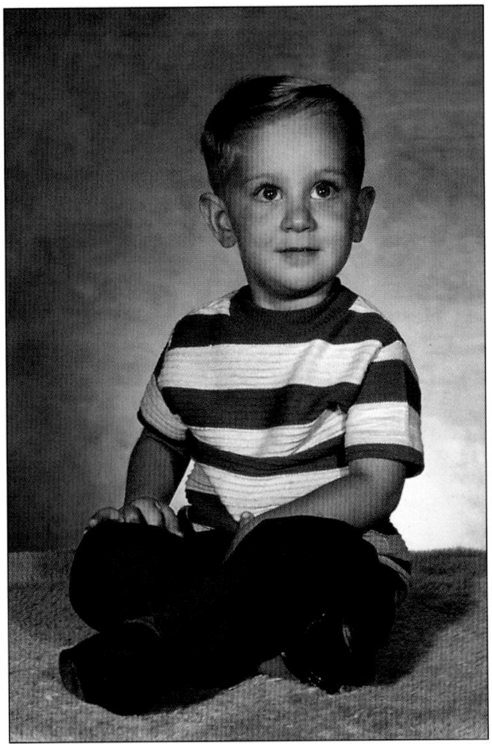

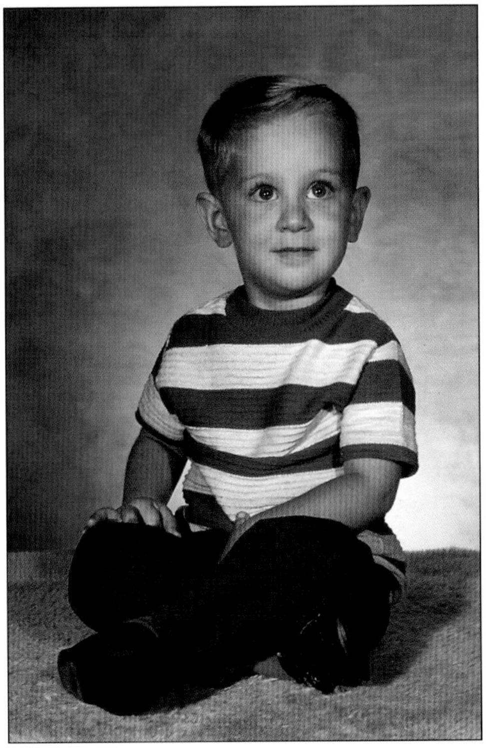

Set White Point

You follow the same procedure to use the Set White Point eyedropper, clicking on an area of the image that you want to be pure white. If there's not a clear choice (like a very bright highlight), try clicking around on the image until you find the best choice. Be careful to avoid creating ugly areas of pure white highlight with no detail. You'll probably also see the color shift to some degree with each click as the colors in the image shift to neutralize the clicked-on area to pure white. You can click as many times as you want.

Set Gray Point

Whether or not you will want to use the Set Gray Point eyedropper will depend on the image. If there is no pure gray tone in the image, clicking on this image with this tool will cause some big color shifts as the tone you click on is set to neutral gray, and the other tones in the image are all adjusted accordingly. If you do have an area that should be neutral, though, this can be a good way to eliminate a color cast.

The eyedroppers won't provide a solution to every problem, but they can be a very useful tool when applied selectively. Keep in mind, you can always hit Cancel (or go to Edit>Undo) if you decide you're not improving the look of the image.

WHOA!

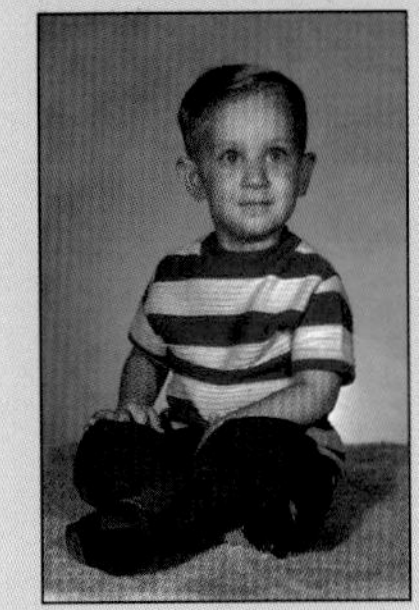

Sometimes clicking with one of the eyedroppers will result in a rather shocking transformation, like a totally bizarre and unappealing color shift. It's no big deal, though. To fix it, just click somewhere else or hit the Cancel button in the Levels dialog box.

SKIN TONES

Because of their vast variety and subtlety of tonality, skin tones are one of the most challenging things to perfect in an image. Often, combining multiple color-correction tools is required to get the results you want.

We see skin tones every day, so we notice it quickly when they just don't look right.

It might seem like this familiarity would make skin tones easy to get right in your photos, but it's not. Skin tones vary widely from person to person, and can change depending on the lighting, activity level, exposure to sun, etc. Skin tones are also very detailed, with hundreds of shades of color rather than a few unified tones. Also, even subtle problems can be very obvious. While you can get away with the grass being a little off-color, it's harder for viewers to overlook skin tones that miss the mark.

Because our eyes "help" us by trying to neutralize the subtle color casts that can make our subjects look bad, it is especially important to use the Eyedropper tool (see pages 54–55) when looking at skin tones. Unfortunately, there is no standard by which to judge "correct" color because there is no "correct" color. The following guidelines may, however, be helpful.

First, you should use the Eyedropper tool to evaluate a median tone on the skin (not a highlight or a shadow). Avoid areas that tend to be pinker (like lips or fingertips) or where there may be shadows (eyelids, under eyes, knees, under chin, etc.). Good areas may include the forehead or jaw area, shins, forearms, etc. Avoid areas where the subject is noticeably tanned (unless the tan is all-over and even). The face is the first thing that most people look at in a portrait, so that's a good place to start.

For fair complexions in daylight, a good starting point would be in the neighborhood of R200/G170/B150. For darker complexions in daylight, a good starting point would be in the neighborhood of R170/G110/B80.

Keep in mind, these numbers are only for reference. If you take eyedropper readings off your subject's face and

The original photo lacks contrast and the skin tones are significantly too blue. The following steps show one possible way of correcting this—but you can combine tools in whatever way works for you. Don't be afraid to use a tool more than once to get the effect you want.

2 The first tool selected was Auto Contrast (top left). This helped the overall contrast, although the image now seems a little too dark.

3 Next, the Levels were used to brighten midtones, and the Set White Point Eyedropper was used to set the white point on a bright white highlight in the frosting (top right).

4 The Color Variations command was then used to decrease the blue and increase the red (bottom left).

5 The Eyedropper tool was used to evaluate the skin tones. This showed that they were still too blue.

6 The Levels were used again to increase the red in the midtones and slightly reduce the blue in the midtones (bottom right).

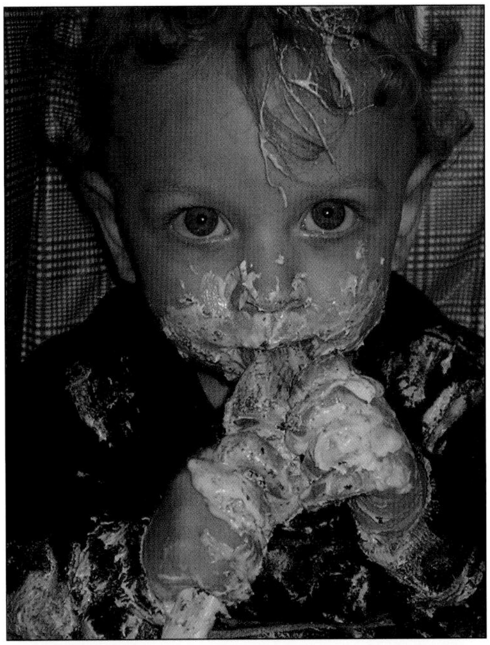

find that the green and blue values are pretty much in line with those listed above but the red is much higher, think about your subject. Is the person's skin actually a little redder than average? Was he or she blushing or flushed? If so, the color might be right on. If not, consider making an adjustment to the skin tones part of your strategy.

Also, these numbers should be considered proportionately, not as absolutes; if your subject's readings seem to be more like R190/G160/B140, that's probably just fine, since all of the colors are just proportionately a bit darker.

Finally, as you move into darker or more shadowed areas of the skin, expect the color to become more blue.

The filters and effects n Elements offer nstant gratification— and some pretty cool ooks for your images. Be prepared to play with these for a while and marvel as they work a little magic!

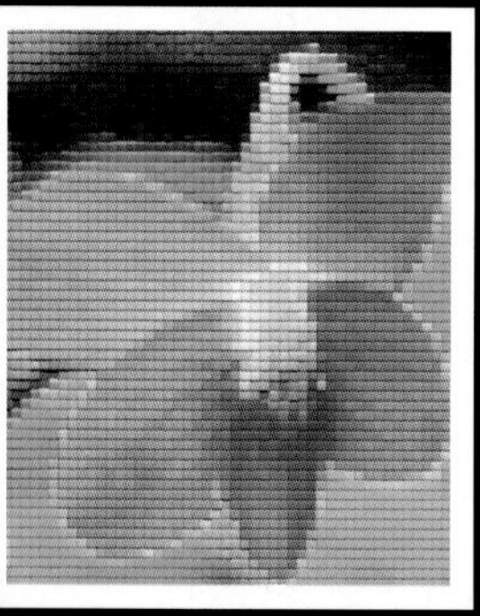

ARTISTIC FILTERS

Getting started using filters is very easy—and the Artistic filters in Elements provide a variety of ways to give your image a very "painterly" look.

A filter is a specialized piece of software that runs within Elements and is used to apply a specific effect to an image. Many filters are packaged with Elements itself, and other filters (from Adobe and other companies) are also available to meet specialized needs. In this book, we'll stick to the ones that are packaged with Elements.

You can apply filters using the Filters palette from the Palette Well. After opening this palette, select All from the pull-down menu at the top to see all of the available filters and a thumbnail preview of the effect of each. When you see one you like, click and drag the thumbnail onto your image to apply the filter. Depending on the filter, this may also open a dialog box in which you can customize the filter's settings.

You can also apply filters by going to the Filter pull-down menu at the top of the screen. Pulling this down will reveal several submenu categories that contain the individual filters. Select any filter to apply it. Some will apply immediately, some will open a dialog box in which you can customize the settings.

To keep things as clear as possible, the filters in this book are discussed in groups according to the way they appear in this Filter pull-down menu.

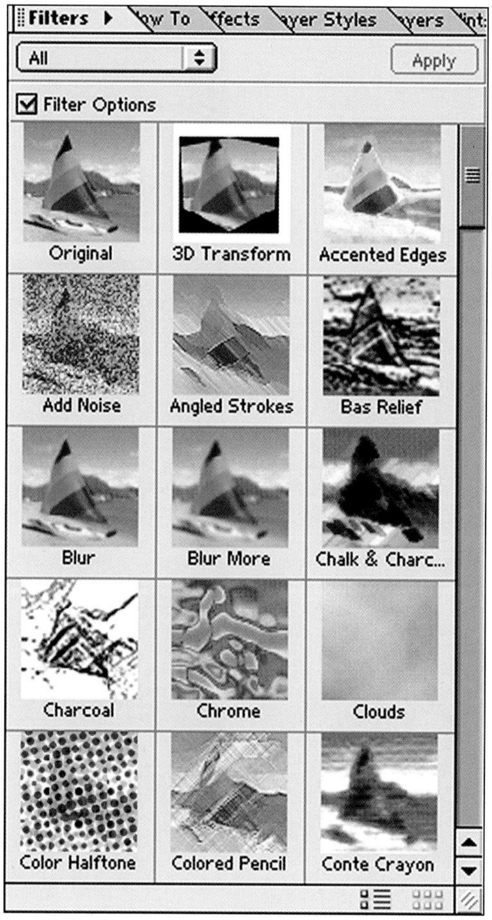

Filters palette from the Palette Well.

Artistic Filters

The filters in this group are designed to imitate the effects of traditional artistic media. For most, you will have the chance to enter settings in a dialog box. A few examples are shown on the facing page. Experiment with these filters and their settings as much as you like—you can always use the Edit>Undo command to reverse the effect if you decide you don't like it.

The filters included in this category are: Colored Pencil, Cutout, Dry Brush, Film Grain, Fresco, Neon Glow, Paint Daubs, Palette Knife, Plastic Wrap, Poster Edges, Rough Pastels, Smudge Stick, Sponge, Underpainting, and Watercolor. Each filter has slightly different controls and effects. The best way to learn to use them is to open an image and begin experimenting.

Original image.

Colored Pencil filter.

Poster Edges filter.

Watercolor filter.

Film Grain filter.

Smudge Stick filter.

BRUSH STROKES AND SKETCH

Don't be afraid to experiment. The filters can produce some strange looks that aren't right for every image, but sometimes the right filter can instantly bring a plain image to life right before your eyes.

With these filters, adjusting the settings in the dialog box will radically change the effect. Spend some time adjusting the various sliders until you find the best look for your image.

Brush Strokes Filters

The filters in the Brush Strokes group can be used to add the look of natural brush strokes to an image. The filters included in this category are: Accented Edges, Angled Strokes, Crosshatch, Dark Strokes, Ink Outlines, Spatter, Sprayed Strokes, and Sumi-e.

When you select the filter you want to apply, a dialog box will appear. In this box, you will be able to set parameters for the length of the brush strokes and their pressure (selections vary slightly from filter to filter). Be sure to use the preview window to adjust and evaluate the settings.

Original image.

Accented Edges filter.

Crosshatch filter.

Spatter filter.

Sprayed Strokes filter.

Sumi-e filter.

Original photograph.

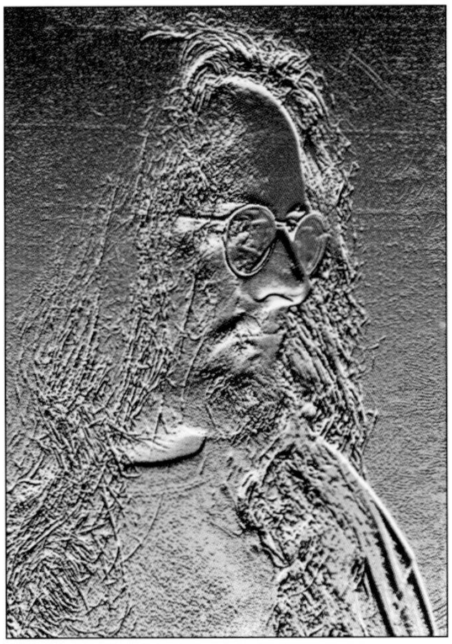
Bas Relief filter.

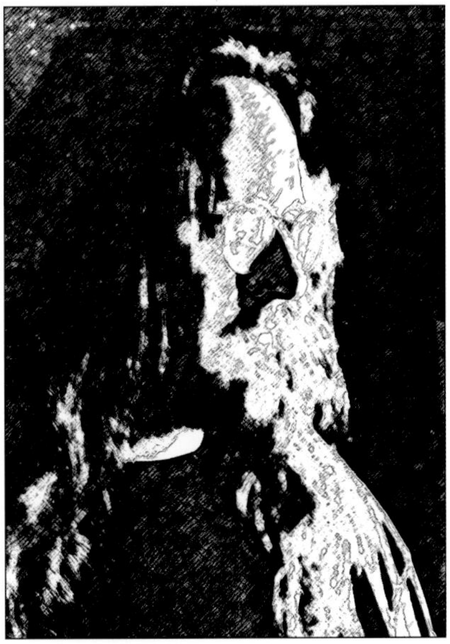
Charcoal filter.

Photocopy filter.

Stamp filter.

Water Paper filter.

Sketch Filters

The Sketch filters imitate the look of the various media used in sketching, as well as some other paper-based artistic processes. These filters include: Bas Relief, Chalk & Charcoal, Charcoal, Chrome, Conté Crayon, Graphic Pen, Halftone Paper, Note Paper, Photocopy, Plaster, Reticulation, Stamp, Torn Edges and Water Paper. The effect of each filter is controlled through a dialog box that opens when you select the filter. The best way to learn about these filters, and the best settings for them, is simply to experiment!

For best results, try using a black & white image. To convert a color image to black & white go to Image>Mode> Grayscale or Enhance>Adjust Color> Remove Color.

BLUR AND DISTORT

You may use the Blur filters with some frequency to soften an image (good for hiding little wrinkles), but use the Distort filters selectively—used too frequently, they can quickly lose their visual impact.

The Gaussian Blur is one of the most frequently used filters in Elements. Read on to learn why.

Blur Filters

The Blur filters let you reduce sharpness in an image. This can be useful for creating a soft-focus effect or for adding special effects (like a motion blur). The filters included in this category are: Blur, Blur More, Gaussian Blur, Motion Blur, Radial Blur, and Smart Blur. Of these, Gaussian Blur is the most flexible, allowing you to create a smooth, all-

Above is the original photo. In the center (top) is the photo with the Gaussian Blur filter applied. Below it (center bottom) is the dialog box for this filter. You increase the blur by moving the slider to the right. On the right (top), the Radial Blur filter is used. Below it (bottom right) is the dialog box for the filter. After selecting the amount of blur, Zoom was selected as the blur method. By clicking and dragging, the Blur Center was moved over the subject's face.

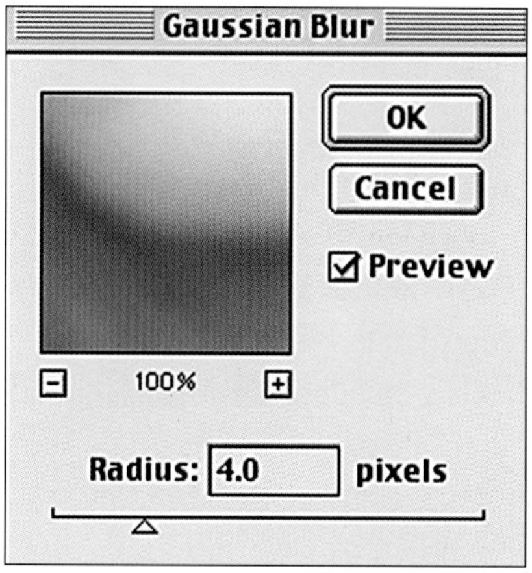

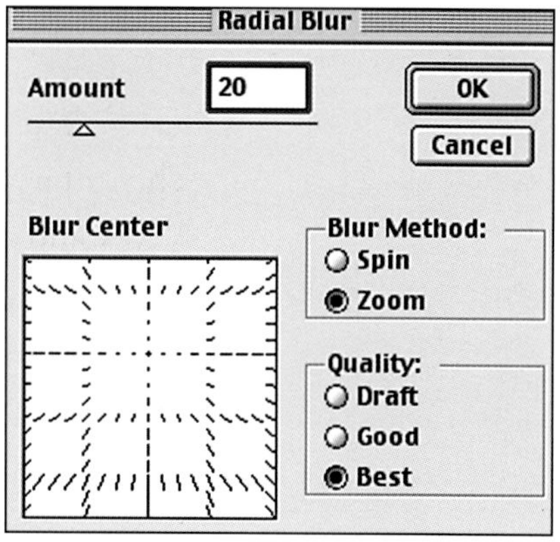

Original photograph.

Diffuse Glow filter.

Pinch filter.

Glass filter (set to glass blocks).

Wave filter.

Zigzag filter (set to pond ripples).

over blur. This is perfect for hiding little wrinkles and imperfections—but a little goes a long way. The Blur and Blur More filters also create an all-over blur, but they don't let you control the intensity. The Radial and Motion Blur filters are useful for creating special effects. Smart Blur softens areas of similar tone while trying to maintain sharp edges.

Distort Filters

The filters in the Distort menu add waves and other effects to images. The filters in this group are quite varied in their effects. The most interesting (and easy to use) of these are:

- **Diffuse Glow**—Applies a misty glow to your image.
- **Glass**—Adds shiny highlights and texture to your image. You can select from the look of frosted glass, glass blocks, etc.
- **Ocean Ripple, Ripple, Wave, Zigzag**—Enhance your image with wave effects (each adjusted using slightly different sets of controls). The Zigzag filter offers a nice pond-ripple setting, for example. Applied to extremes, all create interesting abstracts.
- **Pinch**—Makes the center of the image appear to be pinched in.
- **Spherize**—Makes the center of the image appear to bulge out.
- **Polar Coordinates, Twirl**—Twists your image either from the center or around an edge point.

PIXELATE AND RENDER

Sometimes the name of a filter doesn't tell the whole story. When you're experimenting with filters, be sure to try extreme settings (both high and low). What happens might pleasantly surprise you.

Like most of the sets of filters, there are some gems here, and some you'll never find the right picture for. Spend some time with the Lighting Effects filters, though—you'll discover some useful and interesting effects with the different settings.

Pixelate Filters

The Pixelate filters create a number of stylized effects. Essentially, these filters function by breaking the image into clumps—circles, squares, and other patterns. When using these filters, you should select a relatively low setting in the dialog box, or your image will become unrecognizable.

The Color Halftone and Mezzotint filters replicate the look of traditional printing techniques. The Mosaic, Fragment, Facet, and Crystallize filters break the image up into cells (geometric areas of a single color) of varying shapes. The size of the cell is set in the dialog box.

The Pointillize filter is probably the most useful one in this set, since it replicates the look of a traditional painting technique. In the style of a subgroup of the French Impressionists (called Pointillists), this filter renders the image as

Original photograph.

Mezzotint filter.

Pointillize filter.

Original photograph.

Difference Clouds filter.

Lens Flare filter.

Lighting Effects filter.

groups of tiny dots of color. As long as you keep the cell size small, your eye will blend these dots together into a unified image.

Render Filters

The render filters produce some special 3-D shapes, clouds, refraction patterns, and simulated light effects. These are mathematically intensive filters and may take a while to apply to your image, so be patient.

- **3D Transform**—Allows you to "wrap" your picture over a virtual cylinder, cube, or sphere (in the dialog box, select the appropriate shape, then click and drag over the image preview). You can view your image from different perspectives using the pan and tilt features.
- **Clouds**—Creates clouds based on the foreground and background colors. The on-screen image doesn't affect how they look.
- **Difference Clouds**—Similar to the Clouds filter, but incorporates data from the image on the screen. (Try applying this filter ten or more times sequentially to create a pattern that looks somewhat like marble.)
- **Lens Flare**—Simulates the washed-out effect and geometric shapes created when bright light strikes a camera lens. Specify the center of the flare by clicking inside the image preview or dragging the crosshairs.
- **Lighting Effects**—Allows you to apply a variety of light sources (from flashlights to spotlights) to your image. This is a slightly complicated filter to use. Begin by selecting a style (from the top pull-down menu). Then adjust the direction by clicking and dragging to rotate the light in the preview of your image. Other settings in the dialog box fine-tune the effect—the best way to learn to use these filters is simply to experiment!
- **Texture Fill**—Fills a selection with all or part of a Grayscale file. To add texture, you open the Grayscale document you want to use as the texture fill.

TEXTURE AND STYLIZE

Wrapping up our look at filters are the Texture and Stylize groups. The looks they create are very specialized, but they can be quite interesting when combined in sequence with other filters.

There are two more groups of filters for you to try before we wrap up our discussion of filters. As you've seen, these are powerful imaging tools—but moderation is definitely called for if you want to use them effectively.

Texture Filters

The Texture filters, as their name implies, add the look of a textured surface to your images. The Craquelure filter creates the look of crumbling plaster. The Grain filter, like the Film Grain and Noise filters, adds a speckled look. The Mosaic Tiles and Patchwork filters add a pattern of recessed-looking areas to the image, creating the impression that it is made up of tiles/patches. The Stained Glass filter divides the image up into uniformly colored areas (cells)—it's one of the more realistic effects. Finally, the Texturizer filter let you add the texture of bricks, sandstone, canvas, and burlap. These filters can reduce fine detail. For best results, select images where the shapes of the subjects are more important than their existing texture.

Stylize Filters

The filters in this group can create some very interesting looks. You won't use them every day, but they are a lot of fun. The Diffuse filter puts soft edges on everything. The Emboss filter works like

Original photograph.

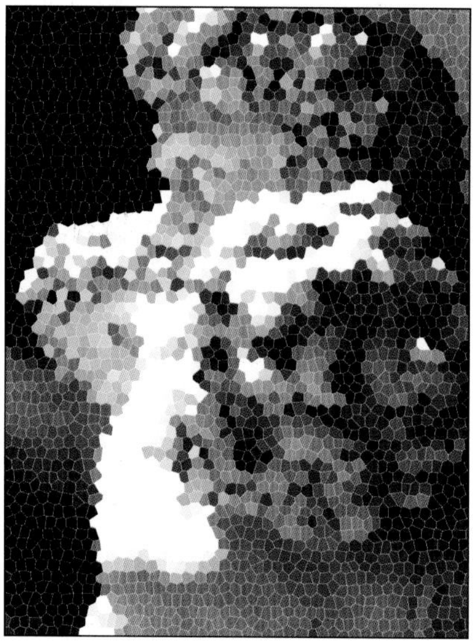

Stained Glass filter.

Texturizer filter (set to brick).

the Bas Relief filter (in the sketch group), but creates "edges" that reflect color. The Extrude filter creates a geometric 3-D look, while the Tiles filter creates a flatter patchwork look. The Find Edges, Glowing Edges, and Trace Contour filters trace the contours of the image with fine lines and can produce appealing results. The Solarize filter creates a stylized look based on a darkroom technique (usually this renders the image quite dark). The Wind filter makes it seem as if the colors are blowing off your photo.

Original photograph.

Find Edges filter.

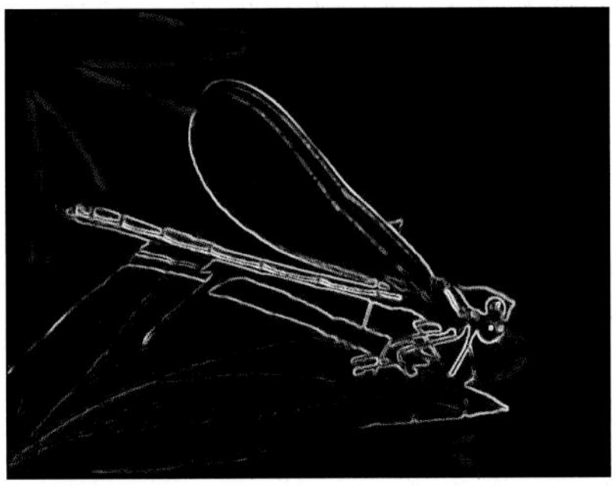

Glowing Edges filter.

Extrude filter.

Wind filter.

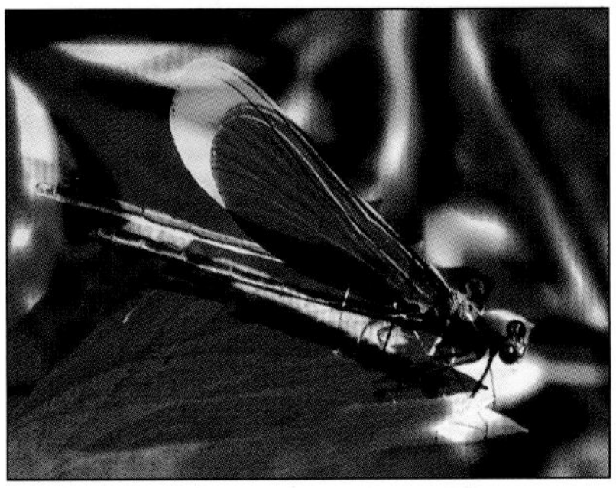

Emboss filter.

COMBINING MULTIPLE FILTERS

Now that you know how to apply filters to your image, don't limit yourself to using only one filter at a time. Using two (or more) filters on your images can often produce truly unique results. There are almost limitless combinations of filters and settings. Here are few you can try:

- Begin with a color image. Run Rough Pastels, then Find Edges to create a strangely colored, crayon-drawn look.
- Begin with a color image. Run the Watercolor filter, then the Water Paper filter for a very textural look.
- Begin with a Grayscale image. Run the Find Edges filter followed by the Smudge Stick.

EFFECTS

Lizard Skin! Green Slime! Molten Lead! Okay, these may not be things you'll use every day, but you have to admit it's tempting. The Effects palette has more practical tools as well, though, so read on.

The effects in Elements work a lot like the filters, but they are significantly more complicated and often involve several steps. Fortunately, all the steps are totally automated, so all you have to do is drag the desired thumbnail icon from the Effects palette (in the Palette Well) onto your image and watch it go to work.

Some of the effects are designed specifically to work on text (see pages 102–3), layers (see pages 82–89), or selections (see pages 90–97). When this is the case, you'll see an "ABC" (for text) across the thumbnail or either "layers" or "selections" in parentheses after the name of the effect. Most of the effects, however, will work on any old image, so give these a try. From the pull-down menu at the top of the palette you can select to view all of the effects at once, or just see select groups, like textures or frames.

In order to accomplish some of these effects, Elements will automatically create layers in your image (these are covered in detail in the next chapter). If this causes you problems when trying to save or work on your image, just go to Layer>Flatten Image and the Layers will be eliminated without changing the appearance of your image.

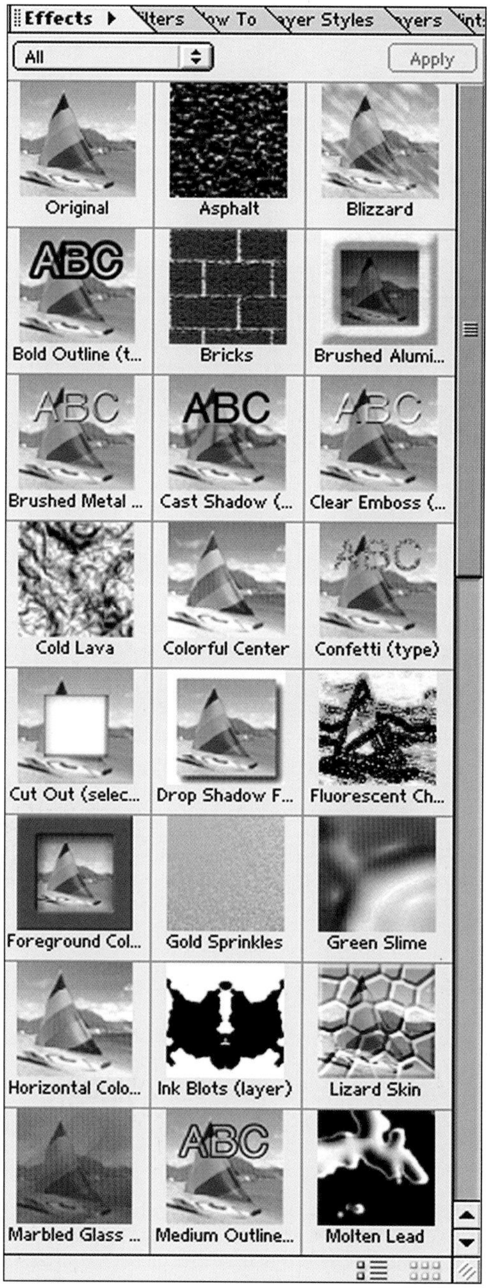

The Effects palette from the Palette Well. Don't forget to scroll all the way to the bottom of the list to check out all the options!

Original photograph.

Blizzard effect.

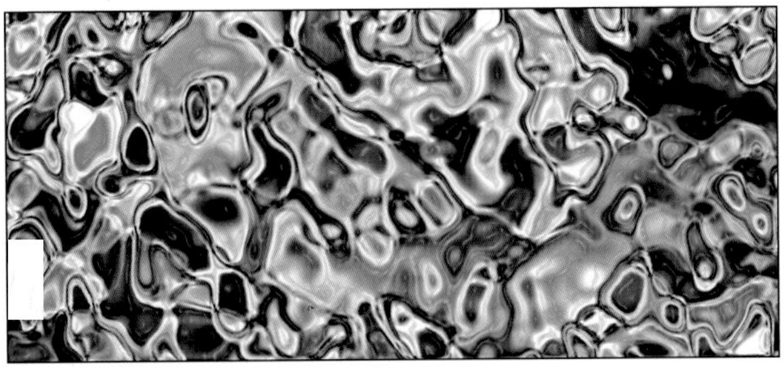

Green Slime effect.

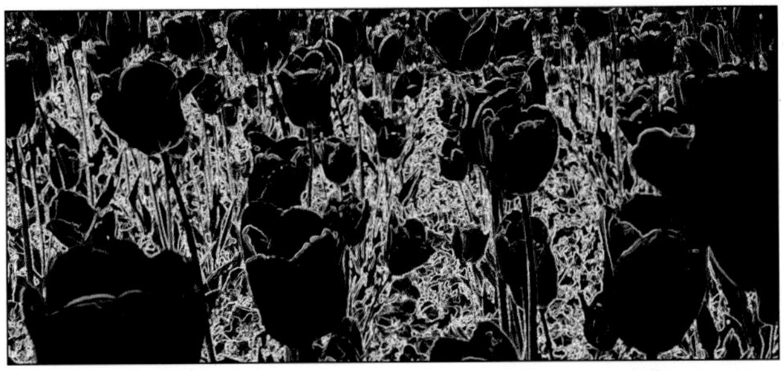

Neon Nights effect.

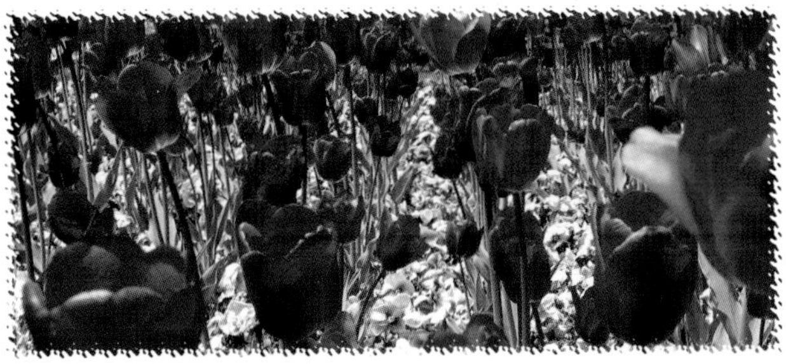

Ripple Frame effect.

Wild Frame effect.

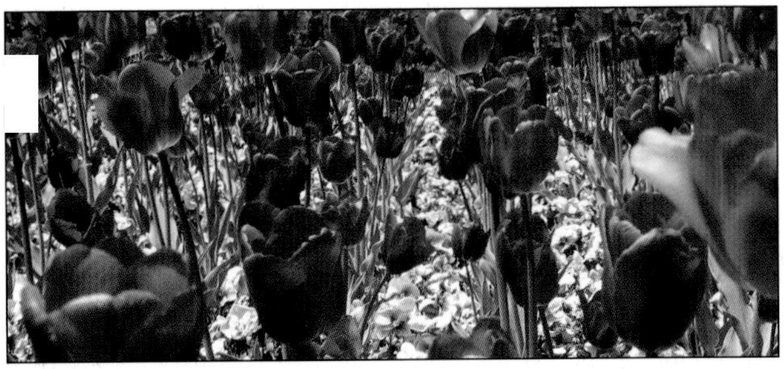

Colorful Center effect.

Marbled Glass effect.

Oil Pastel effect.

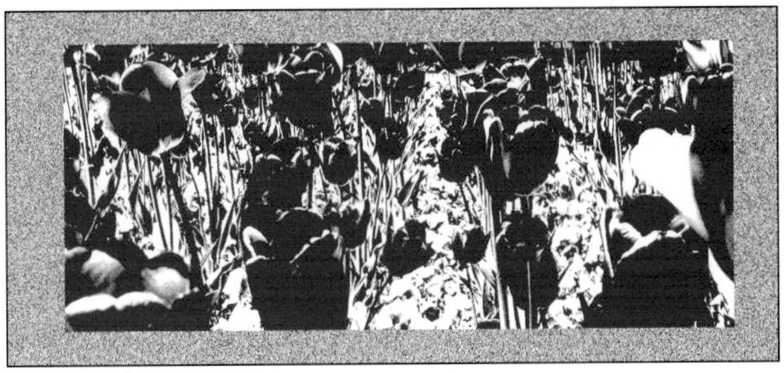

Rubber Stamp effect.

CHAPTER EIGHT

Working with Layers

Master the use of layers and you'll have a brand-new world of imaging options. The more you practice with these, the more intuitive they become, so don't get frustrated—this is a challenging topic!

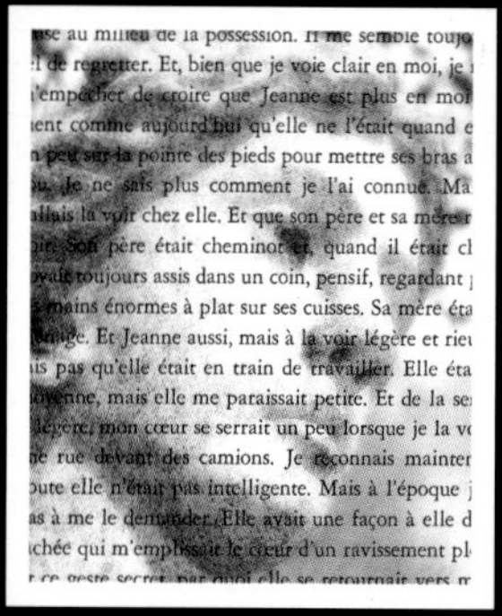

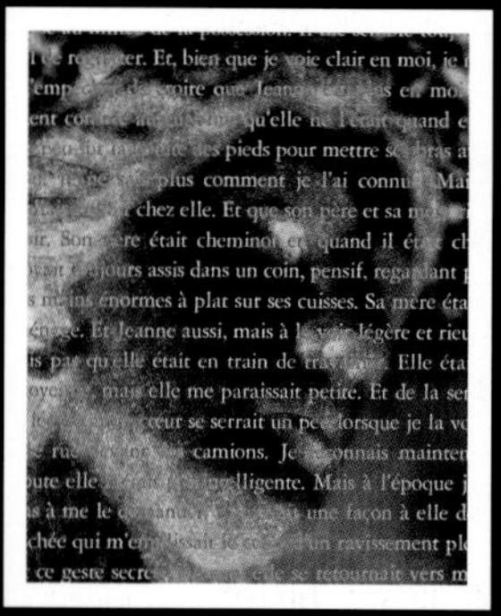

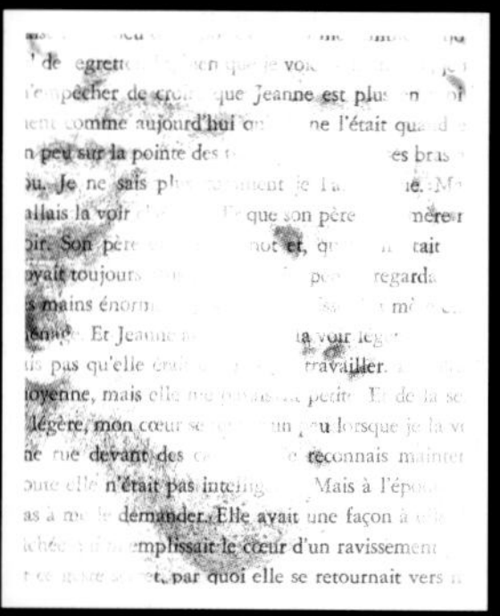

THE BASICS OF LAYERS

Layers are one of the most versatile tools in Elements, making digital imaging even more foolproof. Hate the effect you used? Throw away the layer and start over!

Layers are like sheets of clear plastic, laid one on top of the other. Each layer can be accessed, worked on, moved, or deleted independently of any other layer. This is great for trying out effects, since you can simply discard the layer if you don't like the results.

Layers Palette

Layers are created, accessed, and manipulated via the Layers palette. If this is not visible on your screen, go to Window>Layers. The window will appear in the Palette Well, but you can drag it onto the desktop. As you can see in the diagram on the facing page, many features connected with the use of layers can be accessed directly from this palette. Other features for using layers are accessed via the Layers pull-down menu at the top of the screen.

The main feature in the Layers palette is the list of layers. These are stacked from bottom to top. The background layer (usually the photograph you opened or a new image you're going to add to) is the bottom layer and the layers that overlay it rise one after another to the top of the palette (the top layer in the image).

While the background layer must remain in the background, you can reorganize the other layers as you like by clicking on the layer (usually to the right of its name) and dragging it into a new position on the list.

Making Layers

When you open an image or create a new image, you'll see only one layer: the background layer. You can create as many layers as you like—but additional layers take up more memory. Therefore you'll need more storage space, and more time to open the image or to perform operations on it.

To create a new, empty layer, go to Layer>New>Layer. Alternately, from the upper-right corner of the Layers palette, use the More pull-down menu (from the arrow) and select New Layer. Doing so will cause a dialog box (below) to appear. At the top of this is a blank space to type a name for your new layer. If you don't want to name it yourself, Elements will label the new layers sequentially (Layer 1, Layer 2, etc.). The uses for the other settings will be discussed later in this chapter.

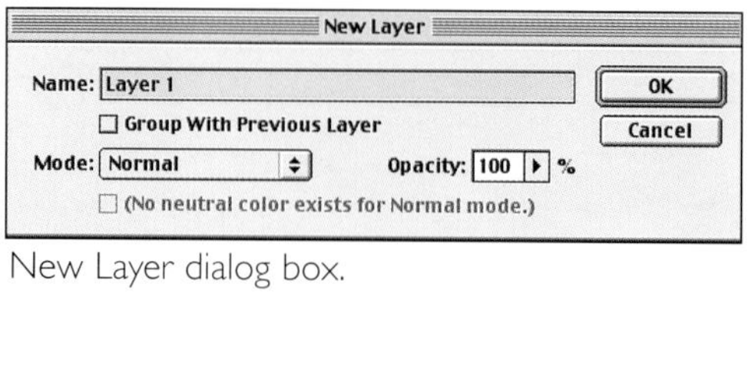

New Layer dialog box.

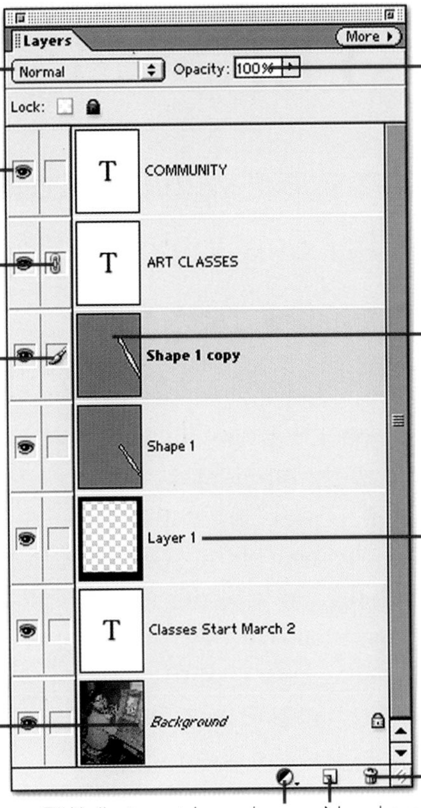

Alternately, you can click on the New Layer icon at the bottom of the palette. A new layer will be created and numbered for you. Its mode will be set to Normal and its opacity will be 100 percent (see pages 84–85).

Often, you may want to duplicate an existing layer. To do this, go to the Layers palette and drag the existing layer onto the New Layer icon. Open an image and try this with your background layer.

You can also create a new layer by dragging in a layer from another image. To do this, open two images and position them so both are at least partially visible on the screen. Choose the Move tool (see page 13), then click on one image and drag it over the other image.

Another way to create a new layer is to select some or all of an image (see chapter 9), then copy (Edit>Copy) and paste (Edit>Paste) it. The pasted area will automatically appear in a new layer.

Removing Layers

To delete a layer, drag it into the trash can at the bottom of the palette. This will remove the layer and any data on it.

To get rid of all of your layers while preserving the data on them, go to Layer>Flatten Image. This will composite all of the layers down into one—preserving everything you've added.

To composite one layer with the one directly below it, select the layer to be composited, then go to Layer>Merge Down.

To composite some (not all) of your layers, make invisible (click the eyeball icon off) the ones you want to preserve. Then, click on a visible layer to activate it and go to Layer>Merge Visible.

Saving Files with Layers

Because digital images are so malleable, you may find that you want to return to an image several times to make improvements. This makes it a good idea to save a working copy of your image before you do any flattening or merging of layers. By preserving the layers, you'll ensure the widest range of editing options.

To save your file with the layers intact go to File>Save As. Then, select the Photoshop (PSD) file format from the pull-down menu, name your image, and hit OK.

For many applications (like saving the file as a JPEG to use online), you cannot have layers in your file. In these cases, save a copy with layers (as a PSD), then flatten the image and save a copy of the image in the TIFF or JPEG format.

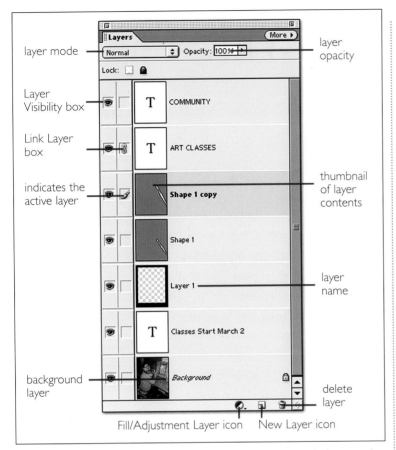

MORE ABOUT LAYERS

This is where layers start to get really versatile—when you begin to control how they interact with each other. Set up an image as described below and give these layer settings a try.

To begin playing with some layer settings, you'll need to create an image with layers. To get started open two images and drag one into the other as described on the previous page. Don't worry if they aren't the same size or look weird together—this is just for practice!

Layer Modes

The layer modes are a predetermined set of instructions for how the layers should interact with each other. To experiment with the layer modes, activate any layer (other than the background layer) with image data on it. Then, use the pull-down menu at the top of the Layers palette to switch the mode of this layer. On the next page is an overview of the differences between modes; this is just for reference. What's important is to get a feel for the looks you can create.

Layer Opacity

A layer's opacity determines how transparent it is (how much of the underlying

Flower overlays leaf on separate layer.

Flower layer set to 75-percent opacity.

Flower layer set to 35-percent opacity.

Flower layer set to Vivid Light mode.

Flower layer set to Exclusion mode.

Flower layer set to Linear Burn mode.

layer will be visible through it). To adjust the opacity, click on an overlying layer (not the background) to activate it. Then, at the top of the palette, set the opacity as you like. At 0 percent the layer will be invisible; at 100 percent it will be opaque.

LAYER MODES: AN OVERVIEW

Normal—No change takes place.

Dissolve—Pixels scatter based on their transparency.

Multiply—The mathematical value of the top layer is multiplied with that of the bottom layer(s).

Screen—The mathematical value of the top layer is added to that of the bottom layer(s).

Overlay—Light areas in the top layer are "screened" (see above); dark layers are "multiplied" (see above).

Soft Light—Based on the overlying layer, treats black as burning and white as dodging (see pages 108–9).

Hard Light—Very similar to the Overlay mode.

Color Dodge—Similar to both Screen and Lighten, tends to lighten images.

Color Burn—Like Color Dodge, but darkens images.

Darken—Chooses the darkest values of the affected pixels.

Lighten—Chooses the lightest values of the affected pixels.

Difference—Displays the difference between the top and bottom pixels based on their hue and brightness.

Exclusion—Inverts colors in the underlying area based on the lighter areas in the layer above.

Hue—Alters the color of the layer without affecting the brightness or saturation.

Saturation—Saturation of upper layer replaces that of lower level.

Color—Colors of upper layer replace colors of lower layer, while brightness remains constant.

Luminosity—Retains underlying layer's color and saturation while basing brightness on the upper layer.

Linking Layers

Often, it's helpful to link layers together. Imagine that (for some reason) you have your subject's body on one layer and her head on another. They are perfectly lined up, but now you want to move them both three inches to the left. You could move them individually and realign them, or—better yet—you could link them. Then, when you move the head, the body will always come along with it (as well it should!).

To group two (or more) layers, choose one of the layers and click on it to activate it. Then, click the Link Layer box (see page 83) next to each layer to be linked to the one you selected. A chain will appear, indicating the layer is linked to the layer that is currently active. To unlink any of the layers, click on the chain again and it will disappear.

Make Visible/Invisible

When you want to work on a layer without being distracted by image elements on other layers, simply make those layers temporarily invisible. To do so, click on the Layer Visibility box (see page 83). Doing so will make the eyeball icon disappear, indicating the layer is invisible. To make it visible again, click the Layer Visibility box again.

This technique is really helpful when the area you want to work on is partially obscured by image elements on a layer above it.

Or, if you're trying to decide between two options for an image, you can execute each option on a separate layer, then switch them on alternately to decide which one looks best.

LAYER STYLES

Layer styles help your layers stand out from each other, creating a sense of depth. This can help you add a nifty three-dimensional feel to your images.

Sometimes you don't want your layers to blend seamlessly with each other—you may even want them to look very much separate. The layer styles will help you create visual definition and add a sense of depth.

To do this, begin with an image that has two or more layers (layer styles cannot be created on a background layer). In the example shown here, a leaf was used as the background and pictures of flowers were added. (*Hint:* The image on the layer where you create the effect should have some free edges [not fill the entire layer edge to edge].)

To apply a layer style, activate the layer to which you want to apply the style (by clicking on it in the Layers palette), then open the Layer Styles palette in the Palette Well, select an effect, and drag it into the image frame.

If you want to modify a layer style, you can access its settings from the layer by double clicking on the "*f*" at the far-right end of the layer in the Layers palette. If you want to remove a layer style you added, first activate the layer, then open the Layer Styles palette, and click on the "⦸" at the top right corner.

The effects of layer styles vary widely, so experiment with them and keep them in mind for future projects!

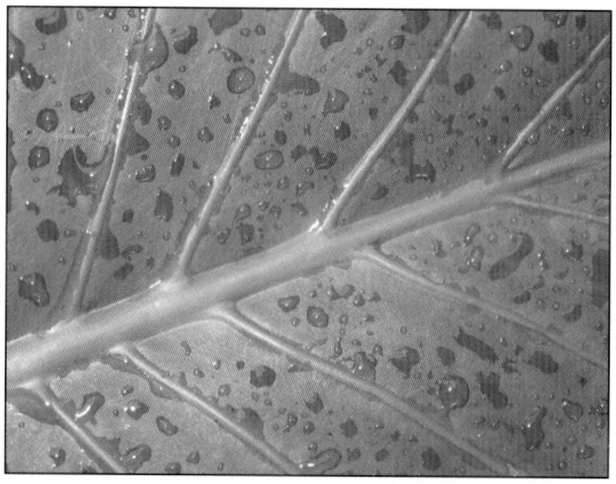

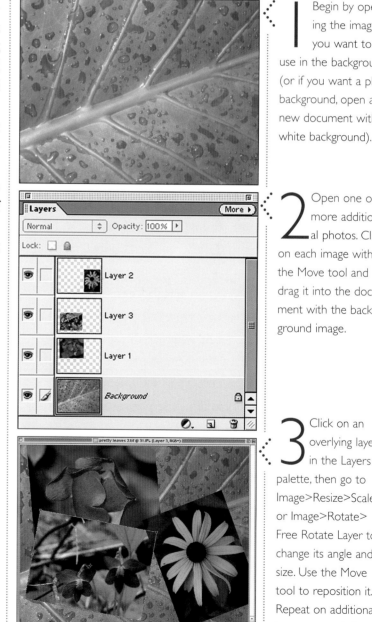

1 Begin by opening the image you want to use in the background (or if you want a plain background, open a new document with a white background).

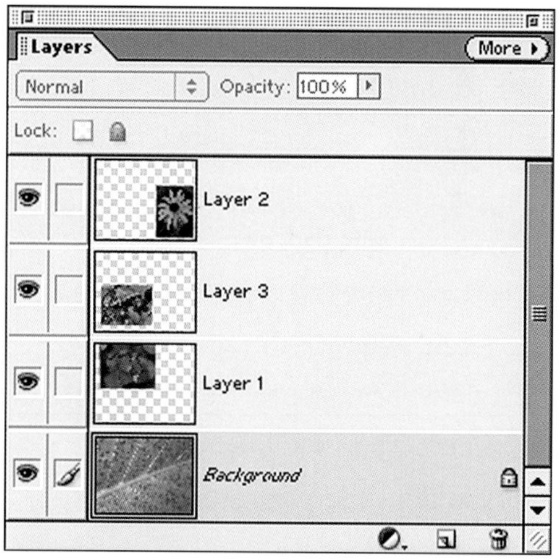

2 Open one or more additional photos. Click on each image with the Move tool and drag it into the document with the background image.

3 Click on an overlying layer in the Layers palette, then go to Image>Resize>Scale or Image>Rotate>Free Rotate Layer to change its angle and size. Use the Move tool to reposition it. Repeat on additional layers as needed.

4 Open the Layer Styles menu from the Palette Well and use the pull-down menu to select a type of effect. From the window below, click and drag the desired effect into your image window. You can add multiple effects to a layer from among the different sets of effects.

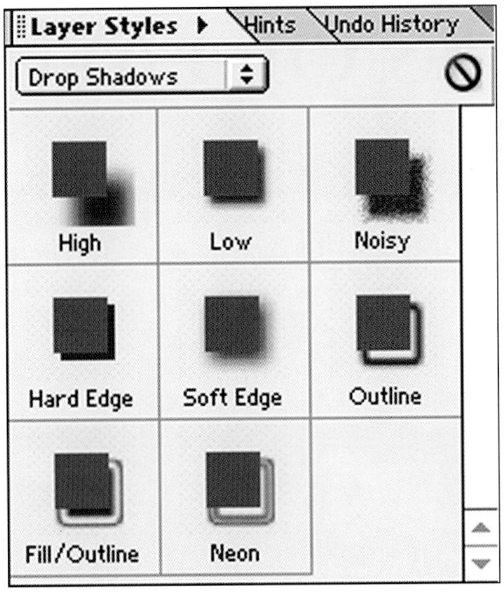

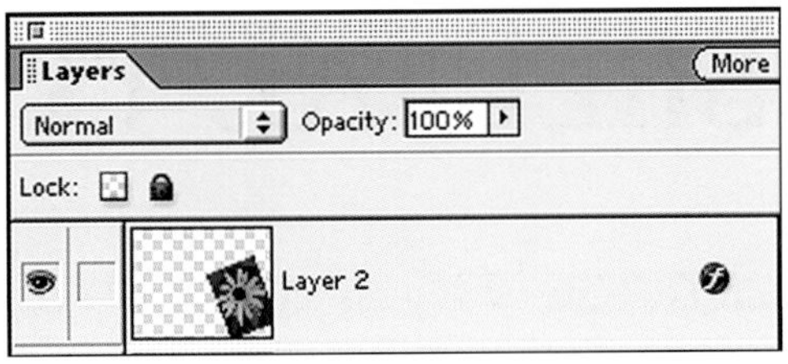

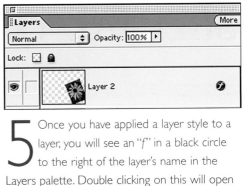

5 Once you have applied a layer style to a layer, you will see an "f" in a black circle to the right of the layer's name in the Layers palette. Double clicking on this will open additional options for customizing the look of the layer style.

Image with Drop Shadows layer style set to Low.

Image with Outer Glows layer style set to Fire.

Image with Complex layer style (Chrome) and drop shadow.

Image with Bevel layer style and drop shadow.

SPECIAL TYPES OF LAYERS

Because they allow you to execute some common tools on discrete layers (instead of on the image itself), fill and adjustment layers give you an added degree of control when correcting and enhancing color.

When you've applied color corrections so far, it's been to the image itself. With fill and adjustment layers, you have more options—and that's always a good thing!

Adjustment Layers

Adjustment layers are essentially hybrids, combining the features of layers with the functions of the Levels, Brightness/Contrast, Invert, and Posterize commands. There are several important advantages to using these on an adjustment layer. First, because the effects are seen on the image but contained on a discrete layer, you can toss the offending layer in the trash if it doesn't look right. Second, because the effect is on a layer, you can reduce the opacity of the layer to reduce the impact of the change—a great way to really finesse your image. Third, you can also change the layer mode of the adjustment layer to make it blend with the underlying layer in useful ways. Finally, you can access the tool's settings on this layer again and again—they don't zero out or return to the default settings when you hit OK.

To create a new adjustment layer, identify the layer you want to modify by activating it in the Layers palette.

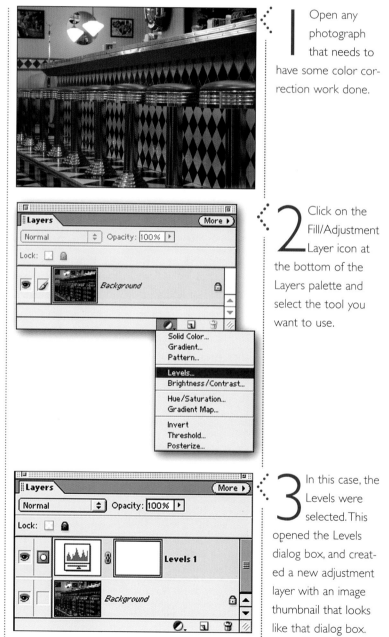

1 Open any photograph that needs to have some color correction work done.

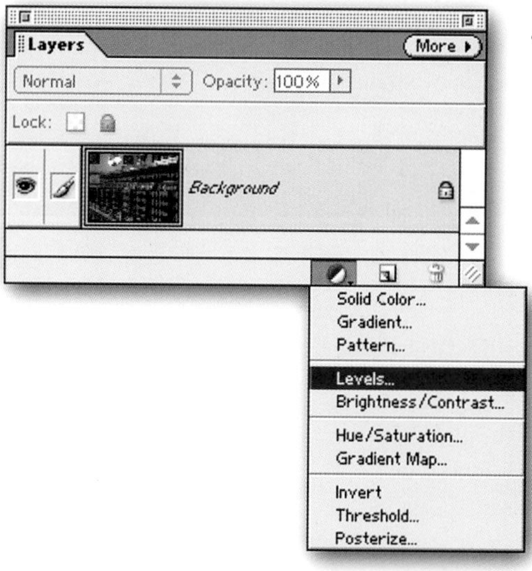

2 Click on the Fill/Adjustment Layer icon at the bottom of the Layers palette and select the tool you want to use.

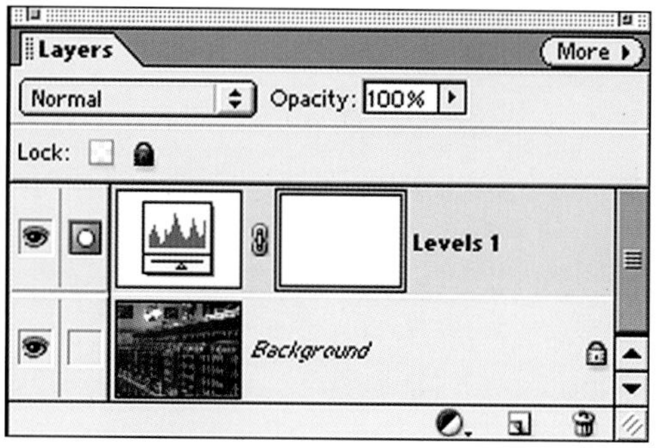

3 In this case, the Levels were selected. This opened the Levels dialog box, and created a new adjustment layer with an image thumbnail that looks like that dialog box.

4 After adjusting the Levels, the color cast in the image was removed (above left). However, the correction seemed to go a little too far; the photo looked cold and uninviting.

5 To correct this, the opacity of the adjustment layer was reduced to 80 percent. This restored some of the warmth of the original color balance by letting it show through the adjustment layer (above right).

Then, go to Layer>New Adjustment Layer and select the tool you want to use from the menu. Next, you will see the New Layer dialog box (see page 82). Enter the settings you want (you can change them later in the layers palette) and hit OK. Then, the dialog box (if any) for the selected tool will open. These work as described in the previous sections on individual tools.

To skip the New Layer dialog box, go to the Fill/Adjustment Layer icon at the bottom of the Layers palette. Clicking on this reveals a pull-down menu. Select the tool you want from this menu, and the dialog box (if any) for the tool will open up.

In the Layers palette, adjustment layers look rather unique. On the left is a layer thumbnail with a graphic representation of the tool used on that layer. If you decide you want to change the values you entered in the dialog box for the tool, simply double click on its icon in the layer. This will reopen the box so you can adjust the settings.

To the right of the layer thumbnail is the layer mask. This allows you to define areas where you do not want to apply the change on the layer. To do this, click on the layer mask icon, then select a brush and paint on the image in black, "masking" these areas. As you do so, the change included on the adjustment layer will be eliminated from the masked areas. To unmask an area (restoring the effect on the adjustment layer), paint over it with white. (See pages 98–99 for tips on painting.)

Fill Layers

To create a new fill layer, you do exactly the same thing, but you can select from three options: Solid Color, Pattern, or Gradient. If you pick Solid Color, the Color Picker will appear, and you can select the one color you want the layer filled with (for more on using the Color Picker, see pages 98–99).

If you pick Pattern, the Pattern Fill dialog box will appear. You can select a pattern from the ones that come with Elements. You can also create and save custom patterns (see page 101).

If you pick Gradient, the Gradient Fill dialog box will appear. From the Gradient menu in this box you can select one of Elements' preloaded gradients. (For information on creating your own gradient, see page 101.)

Thought you had powerful control over your images with the tools presented so far? Surprise! When you master selections, you can start to make the precise changes needed to really perfect your images.

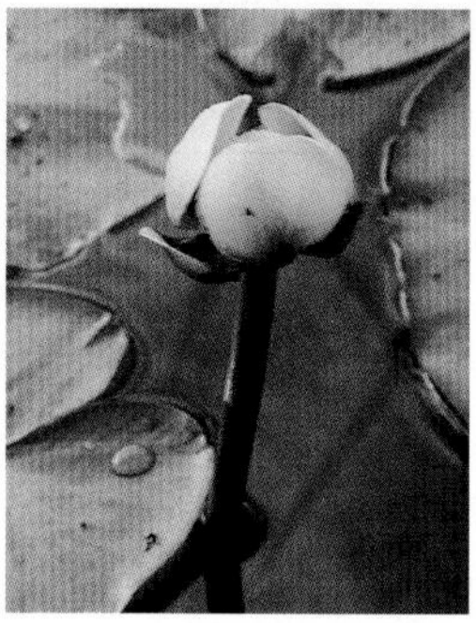

BASICS AND TOOLS

Selections are all about localized control—changing just the part of the image that needs work, or making totally different changes to different parts of the image.

So far, the techniques discussed have been applied to the entire image. The selection tools allow you to isolate individual areas that need work and apply your changes to only those areas.

When using selection tools, the areas you have selected are indicated by a flashing dotted black & white line (often called "marching ants") around the area. Making this line fall exactly where you want it to is the key to making accurate selections.

The selection tools also have unique Options bars (see page 13) that allow them to be customized for each task. As we begin to use these tools individually, you will learn how to adjust the options and how the versatility of each tool improves your ability to work with images.

Note: Once you have made a selection, *do not* click anywhere else on your image with a selection tool unless you want to deactivate (eliminate) your selection. If you accidentally do this, use the Undo Histories to undo it.

Select All

The simplest way to make a selection (of your whole image) is to go to Select> All. Try this just to see what the selection indicator looks like.

Marquee Tool

The Marquee tool (see page 13) is used to make rectangular or elliptical selections. In the Tool bar, click and hold on the Marquee tool icon to make both options visible. Select the tool that best matches the area you want to select, then click and drag over the desired image area to select it. You'll probably need to practice this in order to end up with the selection exactly where you want it in your image. This is especially true with the Elliptical Marquee tool, which can be tricky to master. (Instead of drawing the shape from its edge, it may help to draw it from the center by holding down the Alt/Opt key before you click and drag.)

To select a perfectly square or perfectly round area, select the Marquee tool (either rectangular or elliptical), press the Shift key, then click and drag over your image.

To make a selection of a fixed size, go to the Options bar and make the appropriate selection from the Style menu. Then, enter the measurements you desire in the boxes next to this menu. Also in the Options bar, note the Feather setting. This controls how sharp the edges of your selection will be. The higher the number, the more soft or

Using the Lasso tool, the pigs were selected. Then their color was adjusted to make them blue—without changing anything else in the image.

blurry the edges will be (although this isn't visible until you start editing the selected area).

Lasso Tool

The Lasso has three variations: Lasso, Polygonal Lasso, and Magnetic Lasso.

The Lasso tool is used to draw around an irregularly shaped area using a continuous line. This line can be made up of any combination of straight and curved areas. To use it, select the Lasso tool, click on one edge of the area to be selected, then drag your cursor around the perimeter of that area.

The Polygonal Lasso tool lets you create geometric selections. To do this, select the tool, then click on one corner of the area to be selected. Release the mouse button, move the cursor to the next corner, and click the mouse. Repeat until the shape is selected.

The Magnetic Lasso tool is similar to the regular Lasso, but it tries to help you make more accurate selections by automatically "sticking" to lines in the image. To use it, select the Magnetic Lasso tool, click on one edge of the area to be selected, then drag your cursor around the perimeter of the area to be selected.

Specialized settings in the Options bar are used to control what the Lasso "sticks" to. Lasso Width controls how important the detected edge is versus the actual path of your mouse. Frequency controls how smooth you are able to make curves. Edge Contrast tells Elements how to decide what's a line and what's not. Be prepared! This takes a good deal of practice to master.

TIPS

MARQUEE TOOL:

- To reposition a selection after you have released the mouse button, select the Marquee tool, then click and hold within the selected area and drag the selection into place.
- To deactivate a selection, click outside the selection with the Marquee tool.

LASSO TOOL:

- You must end the selection where you began it (make a closed shape).
- To draw a perfectly straight horizontal or vertical line, press and hold the Shift key while you are tracing the edge of your selection.

MORE SELECTION TOOLS

Don't think about the selection tools in isolation. To make the most accurate selections (which yield the best-looking results), you'll almost always need to use more than one tool.

The selection tools discussed in the previous chapter allowed you to make your selections geometrically or by drawing them onto the image. The following tools offer a different approach that often works well in concert with the previously discussed tools.

Magic Wand

The Magic Wand is a selection tool that is used to select areas based on their color. It is very useful when you need to select an irregularly shaped area with little or no tonal variations (like the blue areas in a sky with scattered clouds).

To use it, choose the Magic Wand from the Tool bar (see page 13). Identify the area to be selected. Click on one point in that area. The Magic Wand will automatically select that point and all other contiguous points of the same color. (To select *all* the points of the same color in the *entire* image, just click to deactivate the Continuous setting in the Options bar.)

For the Magic Wand, the most important options setting is Tolerance. By setting the Tolerance, you can define how picky Elements will be in defining what colors are "the same" as the one you indicated (and, therefore, what will be included in the selection). The larger the number you enter, the more liberal its definition will be. A good place to start is at about 30. Often, you'll need to experiment to determine the value that works best. To do this, simply enter a value and click on the area you want to select. If you want to expand the area, enter a larger value, then click on the area again. If you want to reduce the area, enter a smaller value and click on the area again. Repeat this process as needed to find the value that produces the best results for the selection you want to make.

The Magic Wand tool was used to select the orange area on the butterfly's wings. Because it was not set to Contiguous, all of the image areas with the chosen orange color were selected.

Selection Brush

Another great selection tool is the Selection Brush. To use this, pick it

To make selections with the Selection Brush, you simply click and drag the brush over the area you want to select (as seen here at the top left of the photo).

1 To make a mask, select an image where you want to change all but a small part. Here, let's say we want to change all of the leaves but not the flower.

2 Choose the Selection Brush tool and set it to Mask. Then, paint over the flower to mask it. If you make a mistake, press Opt/Alt and "unpaint" the area you didn't want to mask out.

3 When you're done, click on any other tool to turn the mask into a selection. If you need to edit the selection further, choose the Selection Brush again to return to the mask.

from the Tool bar and simply paint over the area you want to select by clicking and dragging. In the Options bar, you can choose a larger or smaller brush size and select the hardness of the brush. (The harder the brush, the more crisp the edges of the selection will appear, although you won't be able to see this until you start making changes with the selection. For more on this, see page 99.) You can also use the Selection Brush to create layer masks.

Masks

Many people find masks confusing, but they are just a different way of making a selection. Masks in Elements are used to cover areas that you don't want to change. Therefore, to apply a mask, you use the Selection Brush to paint over the area of the image that you *don't* want to select. For that reason, it's a good tool to choose when you want to select all but a small area of an image.

When you switch over to the Mask mode, you'll see the brush options as noted for the Selection Brush, plus two additional options in the Options bar. The Overlay Color is the color that you will paint the mask with and is set to red by default; the Overlay Opacity lets you control how much of your image shows through the mask. Because of this overlay, you'll be able to see how soft or hard the edges of your selection are (controlled by the brush's hardness).

Painting a bunch of bright red brush strokes onto your image may seem a little scary, but not to worry—they disappear and leave a standard selection indicator around the unpainted area as soon as you are done and pick another tool.

MODIFYING SELECTIONS

Once you have a selection made, are you stuck with it? No way! You can add to it, subtract from it, expand it, smooth it—and do a lot of other things to make it precisely the way you want it.

In addition to helping us when we can't trace the perfect shape with our mouse, modifying selections helps us be strategic about making selections.

Adding/Subtracting

To add to a selection (include more image within it), choose a selection tool. In the Options bar, click on the Add to Selection icon. A "+" will appear next to your cursor, indicating that you are now adding to the selection. (Holding the Shift key will also set the tool to add to a selection.) Use the tool to select the area you want to add. It's okay if the new area overlaps the previously selected areas; the overlaps will be combined in the new selection.

To subtract from a selection (cut from the existing selection), choose a selection tool and click on the Subtract from Selection icon. A "–" will appear next to your cursor, indicating that you are subtracting from the selection. Select the area you want to remove from your selection. (Holding the Opt/Alt key will also set the tool to subtract from a selection.)

Inversing

Inversing a selection (Select>Inverse) selects all of the areas that are *not* in the current selection. This is a useful tool in two common situations.

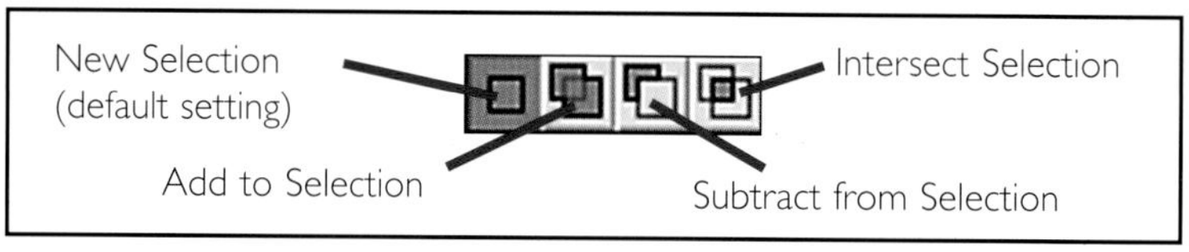

First, imagine a portrait that needs only small color corrections—except for the subject's shirt, which should be a totally different color. You can select the shirt, change the color, then inverse the selection and make the other changes.

Second, in some instances it is easier to select the material you *don't* want to select, then inverse the selection to include the areas you *do* want. For example, when you want to select a

SAVING AND LOADING

Making complicated selections takes some time—especially when you are new to the process. When you have finished making one, you can save it by going to Selection>Save Selection. In the dialog box, name your selection and make sure New Selection is chosen. Then hit the OK button. If you need to reuse the selection, just go to Selection>Load Selection and choose the selection you named from the pull-down menu at the top of the dialog box that appears.

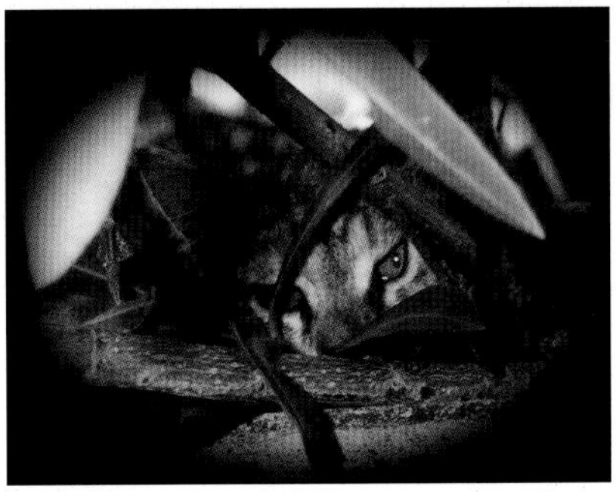

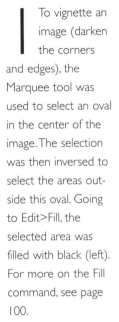

1 To vignette an image (darken the corners and edges), the Marquee tool was used to select an oval in the center of the image. The selection was then inversed to select the areas outside this oval. Going to Edit>Fill, the selected area was filled with black (left). For more on the Fill command, see page 100.

2 The edges of the vignette looked hard, so the Undo History palette was used to undo the fill and the selection was feathered 50 pixels (center) before reapplying the Fill command.

3 Step two was repeated, but the selection was feathered 100 pixels to make the vignette even softer (right).

subject who was photographed against a solid background, you can use the Magic Wand to select the solid background, then inverse the selection to select the subject instead.

Feathering

When using the selection tools, you may notice that the edges of the selected area are very hard and abrupt. In photos, this can make the edges of your selection look unnatural—as though they were cut with a pair of scissors. Feathering a selection allows you to slightly (or dramatically) blur the edges of the selected area, creating a smoother look.

To feather an active selection, just go to Select>Feather and enter the desired value in the dialog box that appears. The higher the value, the blurrier the edges of the selection. Deciding exactly what number to enter will take some experimentation. In general, 2 pixels will create an edge that is barely blurred—just enough to create a smooth transition, but not enough to be noticeable to the viewer.

Select>Modify

With a selection made (and still active with the dotted black & white line surrounding it), go to Select>Modify and choose the option you want (Border, Expand, Contract, or Smooth). In the dialog box that appears, select the degree of change by entering a number of pixels (the higher the number, the greater the change). Experimenting with the settings will give you a good idea of what to anticipate. Smoothing a selection by one or two pixels can be particularly useful—especially if you don't have a perfectly steady hand when using the Lasso tool.

Grow

The Grow command allows you to increase an already selected area. It does this by causing the selection to include similar tones in contiguous areas. To apply the Grow command to an active selection, go to Select>Grow. The selection will grow automatically. You can do this repeatedly to make your selection grow incrementally larger.

Similar

The Similar command also allows you to add to your selection. Rather than adding similar contiguous tones, the Similar command seeks out similar tones throughout the image and adds them to your selection. To use the Similar command on an active selection, go to Select>Similar. The selection will grow automatically.

WORKING WITH SELECTIONS

Okay, you've made some selections. Now what? Well, this is where things start to get really interesting—where you start being able to exercise complete control over even the minute details of your image.

If you're like most photographers, you don't shoot a lot of *absolutely perfect* images. Most of us take a lot of *good* pictures—pictures we'd like a lot more if we could fix just one or two little things.

When you start working with selections, you can isolate the changes you make—meaning you can adjust only the parts of the image that bother you and leave the rest alone.

The following are some common operations using selections. These employ some of the techniques you know how to use already and some you'll be learning in the next two chapters.

Distracting Backgrounds

Who doesn't have a bunch of family photos like this sitting around? We keep them because the subject looks good, but don't frame them because, well, nothing else really does.

To eliminate background problems, select the background (using whatever selection tools you want), then make whatever adjustments you decide are needed to improve the situation. This could include applying filters, using the Brightness/Contrast command to darken the area, applying the Clone Stamp tool to stamp out problem areas (see pages 104–5), etc. But whatever tool you want to use, you won't have to worry about messing up the subjects; the selection will constrain your changes to the background.

1 In the image shown here, there's a lot of stuff in the background—a trellis, part of a tent, and somebody's hat on the far right.

2 The background was selected using the Lasso tool. The Gaussian Blur filter was used on the selected area and its contrast and brightness were reduced.

3 Blurring helped, but not quite enough. Therefore, the Clone Stamp tool was used to eliminate the distractions—and the selection helped to ensure that the subjects remained unaltered.

Using a selection made with the Magic Wand tool, the pink color in the dress (left) was isolated from the rest of the image. This allowed it to be changed to any other color (center, right) without affecting any of the other areas of the image.

Changing Colors

On page 46 we looked at the Hue/Saturation command, which can be used to change one color to another. By itself, this is very effective if the color you want to change appears nowhere other than where you want to change it. What happens, though, when you want to change a pink dress to a blue dress, but you don't want the pink purse to change color at the same time? The answer (as you have probably already guessed) is that you make a selection.

Once you've selected the area where you want to change the color, you can use whatever tool or command you want to execute the change—and it will only affect the selected area.

Compositing Images

Imagine you have two almost identical pictures of your friend Susan. In one, Susan is posed in a very flattering way—but she blinked during the exposure! In the other, her eyes are open and she's showing her great smile—but she put her hand in her pocket and it doesn't look as good.

To fix the problem and create one great image, you could select the head from the image where her face looks great, copy the selected area, then paste it into the image where the pose is great.

This technique is called compositing, and it is covered in detail on pages 118–19.

SELECTION TIPS

- To automatically create a new layer, make a selection, then go to Edit>Cut or Edit>Copy (cutting removes the area, copying duplicates it). Then, go to Edit>Paste. The material you paste will reappear on a new layer.
- When you are done with a selection, deselect it by clicking outside it with the Marquee tool or go to Select>Deselect. To reactivate your latest selection, go to Select>Reselect.

Ready to get a little creative? Try adding some original artwork to your photograph or designing a whole new image on a blank canvas. Your imagination is the only limit.

COLORS AND BRUSHES

As any good artist knows, the first step to creating artwork is knowing your tools—and Elements puts a great artistic tool kit right at your fingertips.

Many of the tools in Elements are used for painting, airbrushing, drawing, etc. When using these tools, you need to be able to specify the color of paint that you want to use. There are several ways to do this.

In Elements, you can keep your "brushes" loaded with two colors—the foreground and background colors. Swatches of the current setting for each color appear at the bottom of the Tool bar (below).

The foreground color is the color actively available for painting or drawing. When you open Elements, the foreground color will be set to black, and the background color will be set to white. However, this can be changed and set however you like.

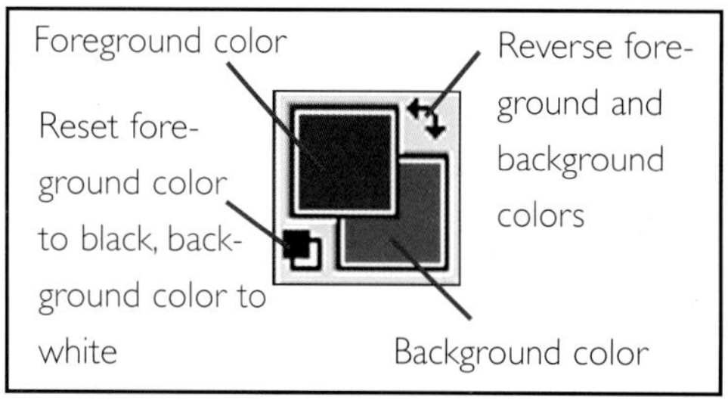

Swatches

The easiest way to change the foreground color is to use the preset colors provided in the Swatches palette (Window>Color Swatches).

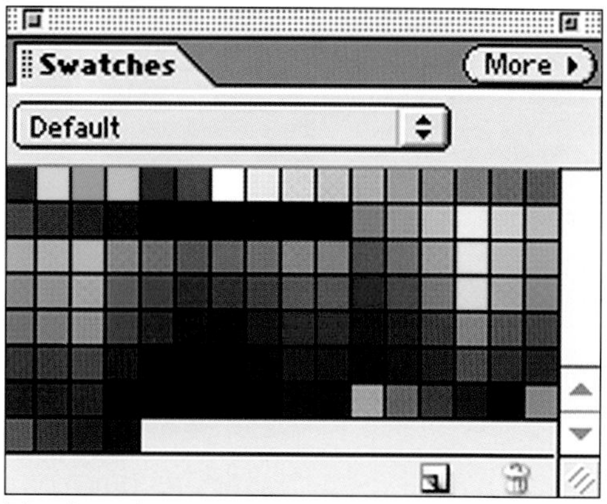

The Swatches palette.

To set one of these colors as your foreground color, simpy click on the square with the color you like. To use a color from the swatches as your background color, hold down the ⌘/Cmd key and click on a swatch.

Color Picker

To create a custom color, use the Color Picker. To open it click once on either the foreground or background color swatch in the Tool bar.

In the Color Picker dialog box, you will see a large window with shades of a single color. To the right is a narrow bar with the full spectrum of colors. At the top right are two swatches; at the top is the current color, and at the bottom is the original color. At the bottom right are the numerical "recipes" for the selected color (see pages 53–55).

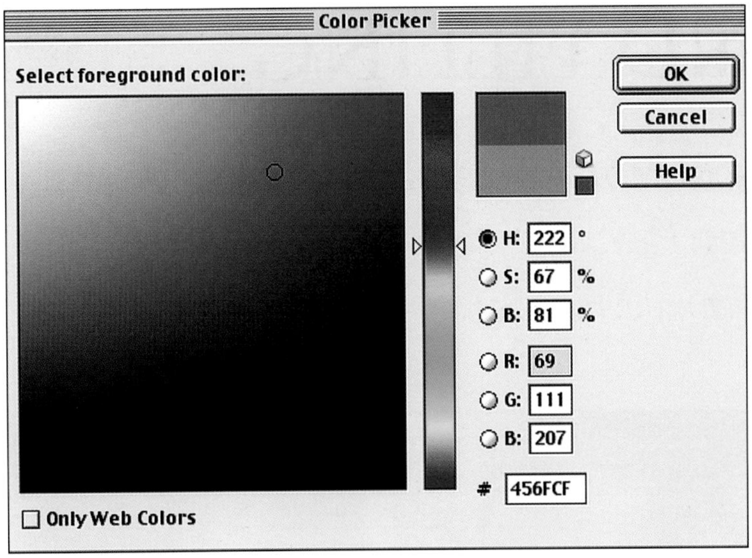

The Color Picker dialog box.

To use the Color Picker, begin with the narrow bar that runs through the colors of the rainbow. Click and drag either of the sliders on the bar up and down until you see something close to the color you want in the large window. Then, in that large window, move your cursor over the color you want and click to select it. Hit OK to apply the change.

To select a second color, use the bent arrow above the color swatches in the Tool bar to reverse the foreground and background colors. This will swap your first color into the background so you can pick a new foreground color. Reverse these as often as you want.

Brushes

When you select a painting tool (see next page), the Options bar changes to include brush size and shape. You can also set the opacity (how transparent the paint you apply will be), and the mode of the paint (identical in name and function to the layer modes—see page 85).

To select one of the many preset brushes, click on the rectangular box with the brush stroke in it in the Options bar. At the top of the window that pops open, you can select from different types of brushes and see samples of them in the window below. To adjust the size of the brush, move to the right on the Options bar and enter a number (the larger the number, the bigger the brush). To adjust the opacity of the paint or the mode, continue to move to the right on the Options bar and set each one as you like.

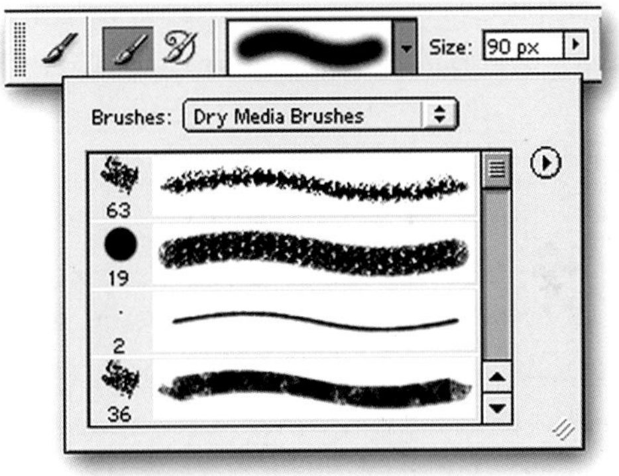

Part of the Options bar for the Brush tool.

When you're done, just click and drag over your image to begin painting with the foreground color you chose.

More Options

In the Options bar, click on the tool icon next the the words "More Options" to further customize your brushes by adjusting the hardness and other characteristics. Consult Elements' excellent help files for more details on these very specialized settings.

DOUBLE DUTY

We looked at one use for the Eyedropper tool on pages 54–55, but you can also use it to select a color from your image for use as the foreground color. Just choose the Eyedropper and click on the desired color.

PAINTING AND FILLING

Painting and filling let you customize your images in ways that were impossible before digital imaging. Play with these tools for a while and you're sure to find uses for them in a number of your images.

The painting tools have similar options but specialized functions, as described below. The fill tools are used to cover large areas, or to fill selected areas with a color or pattern.

Brush and Pencil

Select the tool, pick a brush, and set the tool options as you like. Then, click and drag over your image to paint or draw with the Foreground color.

Impressionist Brush

The Impressionist Brush adds a stylized effect to your image. To use it, you'll still select a brush, as you would with the Brush tool, but your foreground color won't matter; this tool draws its colors from your image. The more times you pass the brush over an area (or the longer you leave it over an area) the more distorted it will become.

Eraser

Erasing the background layer removes data to let the background color show through. Erasing an overlying layer lets the underlying layer show through.

Sponge

The Sponge tool has two modes in the Options bar: Saturate (increase the color intensity) and Desaturate (decrease the color intensity). To use this tool, select the option you want, then move your brush over the image and "paint" the change over the desired area.

The background was selected (ensuring the painting would not affect the subject) and the Impressionist Brush was used to distort it.

Fill

To fill an area with a color, go to Edit> Fill. If you have an active selection, it will be filled; if not, the whole image area will be filled. From the bottom of the Fill dialog box, you can select the fill mode and opacity. From the Contents menu, you can choose to fill with either the foreground color, the background color, black, white, 50-percent gray, or even a pattern.

The Fill dialog box.

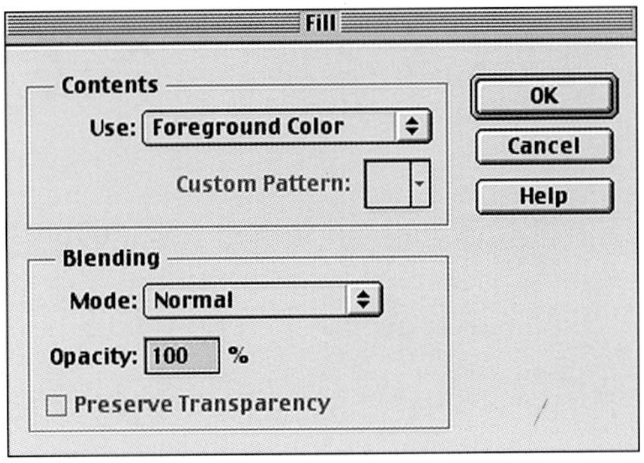

Patterns

To fill with a pattern, go to Edit>Fill, select Pattern from the Contents menu, and click the Custom Pattern thumbnail to view the existing patterns. To create a custom pattern, close the Fill box and select an area of your image. Then, go to Edit>Define Pattern. In the dialog box that appears, name your pattern and hit OK. When you return to the Custom Pattern thumbnail in the Fill dialog box, the new pattern will be listed.

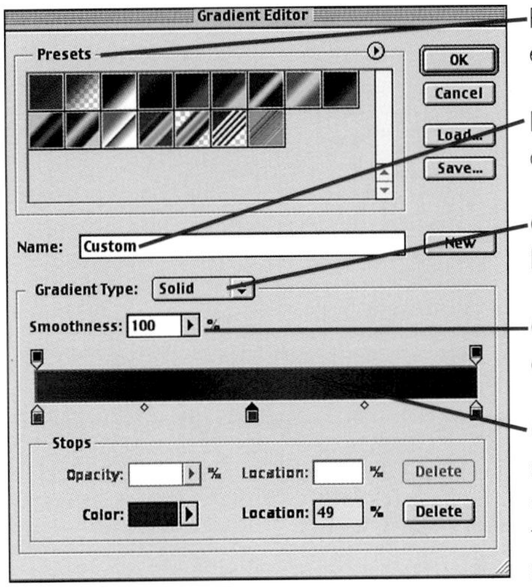

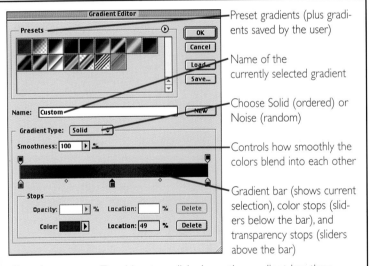

Preset gradients (plus gradients saved by the user)

Name of the currently selected gradient

Choose Solid (ordered) or Noise (random)

Controls how smoothly the colors blend into each other

Gradient bar (shows current selection), color stops (sliders below the bar), and transparency stops (sliders above the bar)

Opacity stops—To add a stop, click above the gradient bar, then drag the stop into position. To edit the opacity in the area under a stop, click on the stop to activate it (turning the point black). Then enter the percentage of opacity in the Opacity box (under Stops).
Color stops—To add a stop, click below the gradient bar, then drag the stop into position. To edit the color of the gradient in the area above a stop, click on the stop to activate it (turning the point black). Then, under Stops, use the pull-down menu to the right of the color box to select the foreground or background color. Or, click on the color box itself to activate the Color Picker, and select a color.

Paint Bucket

The Paint Bucket is like a combination of the Magic Wand and the Fill command. To use it, set the Tolerance in the Options bar (see page 92) and click on the area you want to fill. All areas of the same color will instantly be filled with the current foreground color.

Gradient Tool

The Gradient tool lets you fill an area with a blend of two or more colors (see the middle leaf on page 98 for an example). To use it, select the Gradient tool, then click and drag over your image and release the mouse button.

In the Options bar, you can determine the style of the gradient and the colors used in it. Pull down on the arrow to the right of the colored window showing the currently selected gradient to reveal Elements' preset gradients. If you like, you can select one of these by clicking on it.

If you'd prefer to create your own gradient, click once on the window showing the currently selected gradient. Doing so will open the Gradient Editor dialog box (left). Experiment with these settings and you'll quickly see how they work.

Moving to the right on the Options bar are five boxes that allow you to select the pattern for your gradient (Linear, Radial, Angle, Reflected, or Diamond). At the far right of the palette are settings for: Reverse (flips the colors from left to right), Dither (reduces the appearance of stripes in the gradient), and Transparency (enables any transparency that is edited into the gradient in the Gradient Editor dialog box).

TEXT

Using the Text tool, you can add lettering in almost any imaginable shape or form to your images. So next time you want to make an invitation or flyer, consider using Elements for a creative look.

To add text to an image, select the Text tool from the Tool bar, then set the options as you like. Click anywhere on your image and a blinking cursor will appear. From here, begin typing your text. When you have finished, click the "⊘" (at the far right of the Options bar) to cancel your work or the "✓" button to accept it. Selecting a new tool will automatically accept the current text. All text is automatically created on a new layer.

Options

Just as you would in a word-processing program, you have a number of options for fine-tuning your text. Accessed via the Options bar, these are (from left to right):

Font Style—Choose regular or another style (the styles available vary from font to font).

Font Family—Select the style of type (font) you wish to use from those installed on your computer.

Font Size—Select a size from the pull-down list or type in your own value.

Anti-Aliased—Smoothes the curves in the letters, preventing a jagged look.

Text Styles—Lets you bold, italicize, or underline text.

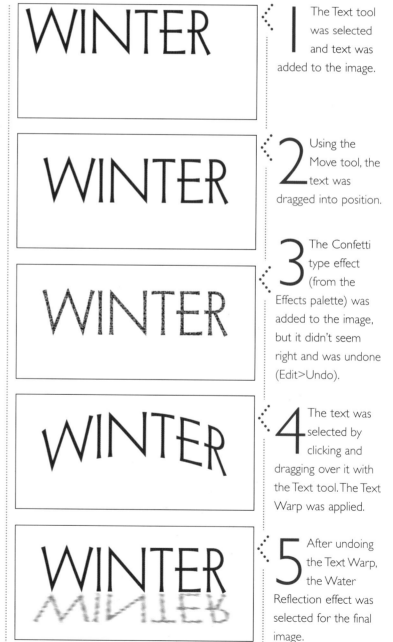

1 The Text tool was selected and text was added to the image.

2 Using the Move tool, the text was dragged into position.

3 The Confetti type effect (from the Effects palette) was added to the image, but it didn't seem right and was undone (Edit>Undo).

4 The text was selected by clicking and dragging over it with the Text tool. The Text Warp was applied.

5 After undoing the Text Warp, the Water Reflection effect was selected for the final image.

In the top image, the word SPRING was selected using the Type Mask tool. The selected area was then copied (Edit>Copy) and pasted (Edit>Paste) into a new file (second image). It could also have been pasted into a new layer in the original leaf image or into another photo. From there, it can be customized as you would any other image layer. In the third image, a bevel was added from the Effects palette. In the final image, the Pointillize filter (Filter>Pixelate>Pointillize) was applied and a drop shadow was added.

CUSTOM SHAPES

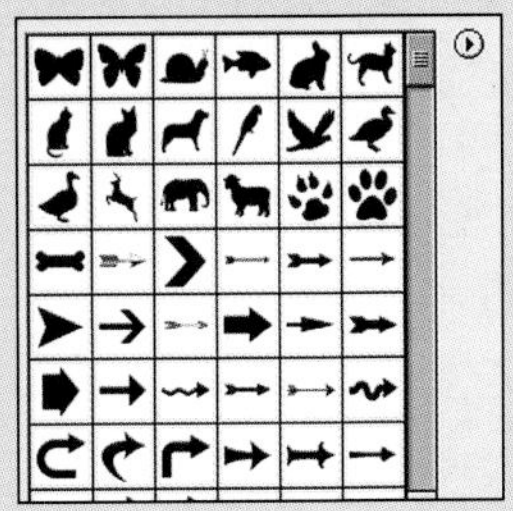

Elements offers a vast array of interesting custom shapes that you can add to your images—there are frames, animals, arrows, symbols, foods, and much more. To add a custom shape to your image, select the Custom Shape tool. In the Options bar, click on the Shape menu (seen here) and pick a shape. (To see all of the available shapes, click on the arrow at the top right of this menu and select All Elements Shapes.) Choose the shape you want to use, then click and drag over your image to add it. You can fill the shape with a color or do anything else you want to it.

Paragraph Justification—Controls how the lines in a paragraph are aligned (left, centered, or right).

Text Color—Sets the color of the text. Click on this box to activate the Color Picker (see pages 98–99).

Text Warp—Allows you to create curved and otherwise distorted text. Simply select the style of warp you want, then set it to vertical or horizontal. By adjusting the bend and horizontal/vertical distortion, you can set the warp as you like.

Vertical or Horizontal Text—Allows you to select whether text runs across the page or up and down it.

Editing Text

To edit your text, select the Text tool and click on the text in your image to reactivate the cursor. You can select strings of text by clicking and dragging over the letters. You can also cut/copy and paste text by selecting it and going to Edit>Cut/Copy and Edit>Paste.

Text Effects

To add some interesting effects to your text, check out the text effects in the Effects palette (see pages 80–81).

Type Mask Tool

Sometimes the effect you want to create with type is better accomplished with the text as a selection rather than as editable text. To do this, go to the Tool bar and hold down on the Text tool. Then choose one of the Text as Mask tools and type your text on the layer where you want the selection to be active. An example of this is shown at the top left of this page.

Image retouching used to be something only professionals could do, but with digital imaging, everyone has the same tools at their fingertips. With some practice, you can achieve the same flawless results!

BLEMISHES, RED-EYE

Red-eye is just one of those things we used to live with in a lot of images—but no more. Now you can quickly remove this annoyance and other little blemishes, too.

Professional image retouching can make a portrait subject look like a million bucks. Now the same tools pros use are at your fingertips, so you never have to live with blemishes and other little problems—even in your snapshots!

The Clone Stamp Tool

The Clone Stamp tool works just like a rubber stamp, but the "ink" for the stamp is data from one good area of your image that you "stamp" over a problem area of your image. Using this tool definitely takes some practice, but once you master it, you'll probably find you use it on just about every image.

To begin, choose the Clone Stamp tool from the Tool bar. Then, set the brush size in the Options bar (the size you choose will depend on the area available to sample from and the area you want to cover). Move your mouse

The Clone Stamp tool is perfect for removing small blemishes (left) and creating a more flawless look (right). You can even use it to remove stray hairs and shape the eyebrows!

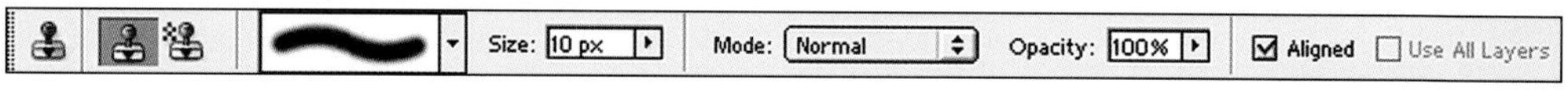

The Clone Stamp tool Options bar.

The Red Eye Brush can be used to remove red-eye (left) and create a much more pleasing appearance (right).

The Red Eye Brush Options bar.

over the area that you want to clone, then hold down the Opt/Alt key and click. Next, move your mouse over the area where you want the cloned data to appear and click (or click and drag). As with the other painting tools, you can also adjust the mode and opacity of the Clone Stamp tool in the Options bar. Don't forget to use the Zoom tool to enlarge your view for precise work.

Red-Eye Brush

Red-eye is just a fact of the anatomy of our eyes, but that doesn't mean we have to live with it our images. Elements makes it easy to remove the problem and create a much more pleasant look. For this correction, it will be very helpful to zoom in tightly on the eyes you want to correct.

To use the Red Eye Brush, choose it from the Tool bar, then select the brush settings you want. Click on Default Colors to reset the Current color to red and the Replacement Color to black. Then, make sure the Sampling is set to First Click. Position your mouse over a red area of the eye and click (or click and drag) to replace the red with a dull gray.

If the red isn't all replaced, try setting the Tolerance slider higher (the default 30-percent setting will work for almost every image, though).

To select a different Replacement Color to more accurately match the color of the subject's eyes, click on the Replacement Color swatch and choose a new color from the Color Picker.

SHARPEN OR SOFTEN

As you work toward perfecting your photos, don't neglect the impact that focus (or a little lack thereof) can have on them. Sharpening and softening are invaluable tools for fine-tuning your images.

Sharpening and blurring are everyday operations with digital images. You can use them to improve flaws in an image or to enhance the appearance of your subject.

Sharpening

If your image looks pretty much okay to the naked eye, but a little fuzziness is apparent when you really get critical, sharpening may do the trick. Almost every scan of an image also requires at least a little sharpening to make it look as crisp as the original. Keep in mind, every image is unique and sharpening decisions are subjective.

To sharpen an image, go to Filter>Sharpen and select the tool you want to use. As noted below, some filters run automatically, while others require you to adjust their settings.

The Sharpen filter automatically applies itself to every pixel in the image or selection. It works by enhancing the contrast between adjoining pixels, creating the appearance of sharper focus. The Sharpen More filter does the same thing, but with more intensity.

The Sharpen Edges filter seeks out the edges of objects and enhances those areas to create the illusion of increased sharpness. Elements identifies edges by looking for differences in color and contrast between adjacent pixels.

Unsharp Mask is the most powerful sharpening filter in Elements. To begin, go to Filter>Sharpen>Unsharp Mask. This will bring up a dialog box in which you can adjust the Amount (how much

The original image was scanned from a print and needed some sharpening.

Using the Unsharp Mask, the image was slightly sharpened.

Sharpening must be done in moderation. Oversharpened photos look grainy and have unattractive light halos around dark areas, and dark halos around light ones.

The Unsharp Mask dialog box.

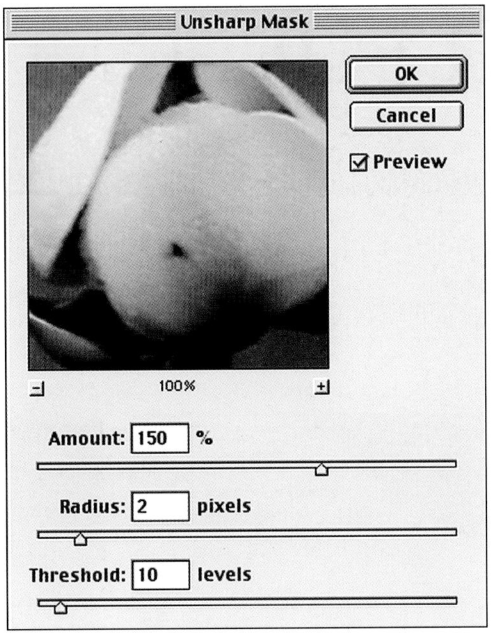

sharpening occurs), the Radius (how far from each pixel the effect is applied), and the Threshold (how similar in value the pixels must be to be sharpened). To start, try setting the Amount to 150 percent, the Radius to 2 pixels, and the Threshold to 10 levels. Watch the preview and fine-tune these settings until you like the results.

Watch out for oversharpening. If you're not sure you've sharpened an image correctly, go to Edit>Undo and compare the new version to the original. If the new one *was* better, use Edit>Redo to return to it.

Elements also has a Sharpen tool. This is used to "paint on" sharpness in selected areas and works pretty much like the other painting tools. The Select field in the Options bar is used to set the intensity of the sharpening effect.

Blur

Images from digital cameras are often so sharp that they don't make people look their best. To add a forgiving amount of softness, duplicate the background layer and apply the Gaussian Blur filter to it (Filter>Blur>Gaussian Blur) at a low setting (3–5 pixels). After applying the filter, set the mode of the duplicated layer to Lighten (at the top of the Layers palette).

The Gaussian Blur filter and the Blur tool (used just like the Sharpening tool, as described above) are also useful for improving images by making distracting elements much less noticeable.

To give a softer look to the original image (right), the background layer was duplicated, blurred, and set to lighten (far right).

DODGE AND BURN

The Dodge and Burn tools simulate classic darkroom techniques that go by the same names. Essentially, dodging lightens and burning darkens—giving you excellent control over the tones in your images.

Ansel Adams was a master in the photographic darkroom. Two of the most important techniques he used are simulated by these tools. While mastering the same tools may not instantly make you a legendary photographer, it will definitely help you make the most of all of your images.

Dodging

The Dodge tool is used to lighten areas of a print. To use it, select the Dodge tool from the Tool bar, then choose a brush (a soft brush works best). Click (or click and drag) over your image to dodge (lighten) as needed.

In the Options bar, increasing the Exposure setting will increase the amount of lightening you achieve. In the Range setting, you can specify whether you want to lighten the shadows, midtones, or highlights in a given area.

This is an important decision, so study the area you are working on carefully to determine the best approach. Often, the best selection is counterintuitive. For example, imagine you have a photograph with a dark shadow area. The area is not solid black, but has very dark gray details. To bring out the details, it might seem logical to dodge

Original photograph.

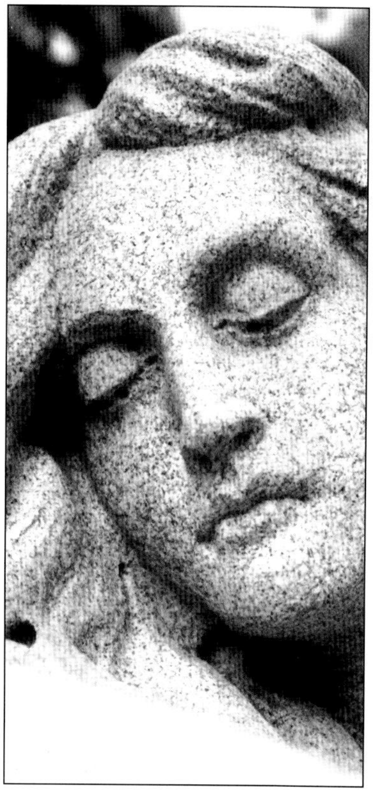

Photograph with 20-percent exposure dodge on midtones.

Dodge tool options.

the shadows. However, in this case, dodging the shadow areas would mean lightening the black areas—making them gray.

If the shadow area and its details are both gray, then the contrast between them has actually been reduced—making the details even less visible. Instead, you would want to dodge the midtones, to lighten the areas that were originally *dark gray*. Making those gray areas a little lighter will make them more apparent to the viewer.

Burning

The Burn tool is used to darken areas of a print. To use it, select the Burn tool from the Tool bar, then choose a brush (a soft brush works best). Click (or click and drag) over your image to burn (darken) as needed.

In the Options bar, increasing the Exposure setting will increase the amount of darkening you achieve. In the Range setting, you can choose to darken the shadows, midtones, or highlights in a given area.

This is an important decision, so study the area you are working on carefully to determine the best approach. Again, the best selection may be counterintuitive. For example, imagine you have a photograph with a bright highlight area. The area is not solid white, but has very light gray details. To bring out the details, it seems it would be logical to burn the highlights. However, in this case, burning the highlight areas would mean darkening the white areas—making them light gray.

If the highlight area and its details are *both* light gray, then the contrast between them has actually been reduced—making the details even less visible. Instead, you would want to burn the midtones or shadows to make the areas that were originally light gray become somewhat darker. This will make them more apparent to the viewer of the image.

Original photograph.

Photograph with 20-percent exposure burn on midtones.

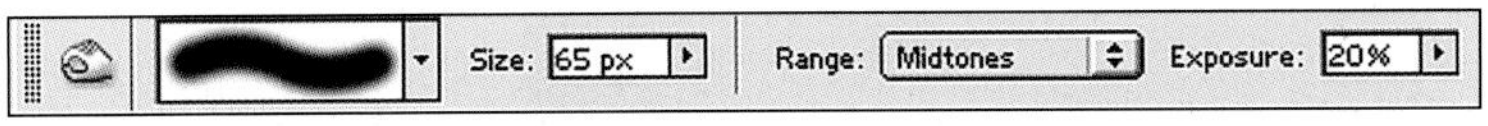

Burn tool options.

TIPS FOR DODGING AND BURNING

Neither dodging nor burning can add detail that isn't in the original image. These tools are most useful for making small changes, such as lightening up a shaded area that's just a little too dark, or making an area that is too light just a little less bright and distracting. You'll rarely get good results dodging a solid black (or extremely dark) area or a solid white (or extremely light) area.

NOISE

Noise, the digital equivalent of film grain, can add beautiful texture to a photograph or ruin an image with ugly speckles—it all depends on the particular image and your artistic intentions.

The appearance of noise is typically associated with the use of high film speeds, but high ISO settings on a digital camera can create it just as well. Typical of the longer exposures in low-light photography (without flash), noise is something most photographers contend with at one time or another. Although noise tends to become visible first in the shadow areas of an image, it's not until it invades the rest of the image (the midtones and highlights) that most people consider it an aesthetic problem.

Reducing Noise

Elements offers two filters (under Filter>Sharpen) designed to reduce the noise in an image (and to remove other small imperfections). Unfortunately, both have significant drawbacks.

DUST & SCRATCHES

The Dust & Scratches filter is good for removing pesky little problems from scanned images. To use it, you'll need to adjust the Radius and Threshold. To start, set both sliders all the way to the left, then click and drag on the image in the preview window until you see the spot or scratch you want to remove. Increase the Radius to blur out the problem, then increase the Threshold to restore texture.

The Despeckle filter relies on the computer to make decisions about what is grain—and usually it won't make the same decisions you would. The result is that, along with the graininess, you will lose some of the *desirable* detail in the image.

Also included in this group is something called the Median filter. This is a

The photo on the far left has quite noticeable grain. The Despeckle filter was used to improve the look of the grain (left)—but detail suffers as a result.

The original image on the left had very little grain. Enhancing it with the Add Noise filter (center) and the Film Grain filter (right) gave the image two slightly different feels.

primitive version of the Dust & Scratches filter. It selects the average (median) color based on the radial distance you select from the dialog box. The higher the setting, the more grain reduction (and the more detail is lost).

If grain reduction in your images is a serious issue to you, you may wish to purchase a third-party plug-in (a program that runs within Elements, usually as a filter) that is designed for reducing grain. Digital GEM from Applied Science Fiction (www.asf.com) is a popular plug-in for grain reduction.

For images with serious grain problems, keep in mind that sharpening should also be avoided (or at least kept to an absolute minimum), as it will make the grain more prominent.

Enhancing Noise

In some images, adding grain creates a nice feel—particularly in black & white images. To do this, you can use the Noise filter (Filter>Noise>Add Noise) or the Film Grain filter (Filter>Artistic>Film Grain). Each of these offer simple controls in their dialog boxes. Make sure that the Preview box is checked in the dialog box, then adjust the sliders until you get the effect you want.

LIQUIFY

The Liquify filter can be used to change the shapes of your subjects. This can be done to subtly enhance their appearance, or to wildly change it—the choice is yours.

Some of the filters in the Distort subgroup were discussed on page 75. There's one more filter in this group, however, that deserves some special consideration. This is the Liquify filter (Filter>Distort>Liquify), which allows you to freely twist, stretch, and warp an image.

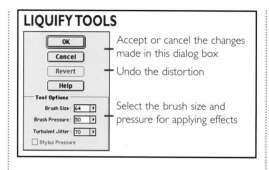

While warping may not sound like an operation that would fall under the category of retouching, it actually does. As you can see below and on the facing page, selectively distorting small areas of an image can help to eliminate little figure flaws in portraits for a more flattering look. It can also be used to smooth out the little bulges that result from tighter clothing, like snug waistbands. In advertising photography, this tool is even used to make a model's eyes or lips look a little bigger or more full.

The key to using the tool for retouching is subtlety. The more you distort a given area, the more likely the

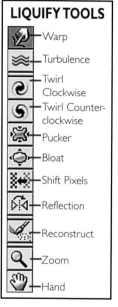

LIQUIFY TOOLS

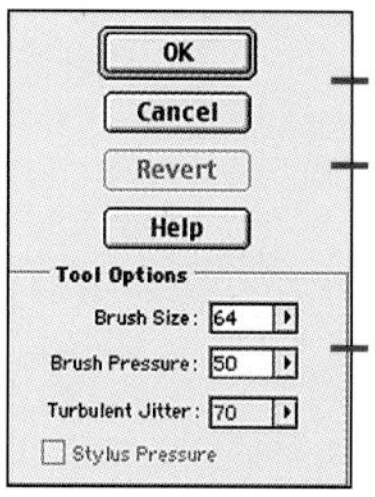

Accept or cancel the changes made in this dialog box

Undo the distortion

Select the brush size and pressure for applying effects

LIQUIFY TOOLS

Warp
Turbulence
Twirl Clockwise
Twirl Counter-clockwise
Pucker
Bloat
Shift Pixels
Reflection
Reconstruct
Zoom
Hand

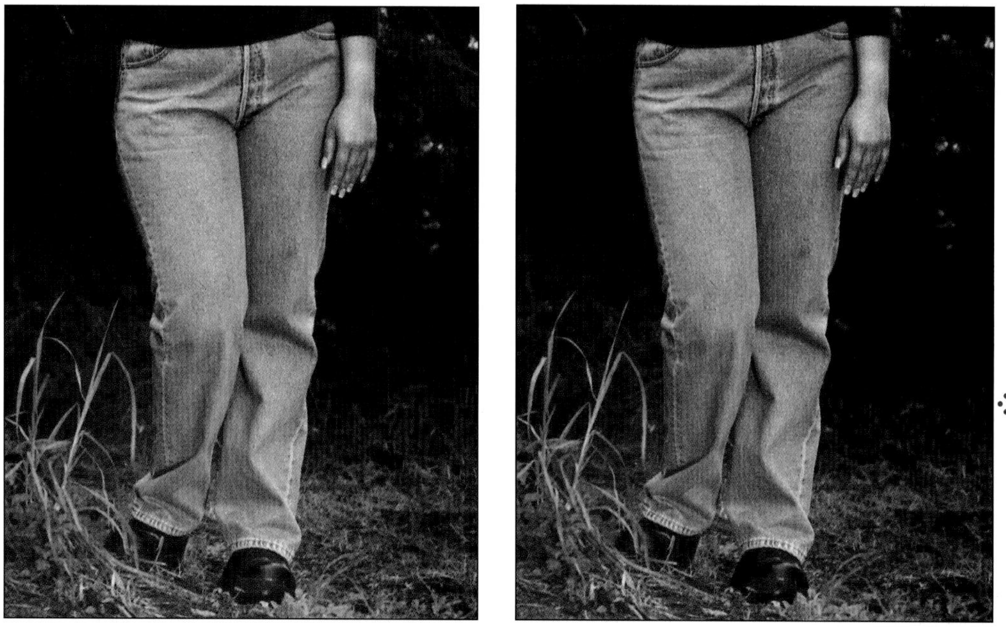

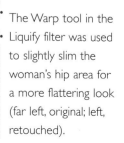

The Warp tool in the Liquify filter was used to slightly slim the woman's hip area for a more flattering look (far left, original; left, retouched).

Here, the man's chin and neck area (left) were reshaped using the Liquify filter (center). Using the Burn tool, the shadows were then enhanced to further reduce the visibility of this area (right). Note that the change is subtle—people should still look like themselves after you make these little refinements.

refinement will look fake. When using it on people, be careful not to distort your subjects so much that they don't look like themselves.

To use this filter, go to Filter>Distort>Liquify. Doing so will open a full-screen dialog box with a large preview of your image in the center and two control panels on either side. To the left of your image are the tools, and to the right are the options.

To begin, select the Warp, Turbulence, Twist, Pucker, Bloat, Shift Pixels, or Reflection tool. Then, choose a brush from the options panel. For the most impact, select a rather large brush (perhaps in the 50–100 range), and set the brush pressure to about 50 (higher settings will provide even more distortion). Then, by clicking and dragging over the image preview, simply begin painting on the distortion. The longer you leave your brush in one area, the more the pixels there will be distorted. Try experimenting with several of the tools, using different brush sizes and pressures, and painting quickly versus slowly.

If you like the results of your work as shown in the preview window, hit OK to accept the changes. If you don't like them but you want to try again, hit Revert.

Of course, the Liquify filter can also be used to create effects that are far from natural!

CHAPTER TWELVE

Simple Photo Projects

Now that you've learned the basic tools and commands in Elements, you can move on to begin combining these techniques to create your own unique digital works of art.

HANDCOLORING

Handcoloring is an incredibly versatile way to really personalize your images—and the effects can be as subtle or dramatic as you want.

Handcoloring photos is traditionally accomplished with a variety of artistic media—oil paints, pencils, etc. With Elements, you can create this classic look much more easily!

Method 1

This technique gives you total control over the colors you add and where you add them.

First, open an image. If it's a color image, go to Enhance>Adjust Color>Remove Color to create a black & white image. If it's a black & white image, go on to the next step.

Next, create a new layer and set it to the Color mode (see page 85).

Double click on the foreground color swatch to activate the Color Picker. Select the color you want and hit OK to select it as the new foreground color. This is the color your painting tools will apply. You may switch it as often as you like.

With your color selected, return to the new layer you created in your image. Click on this layer in the Layers palette

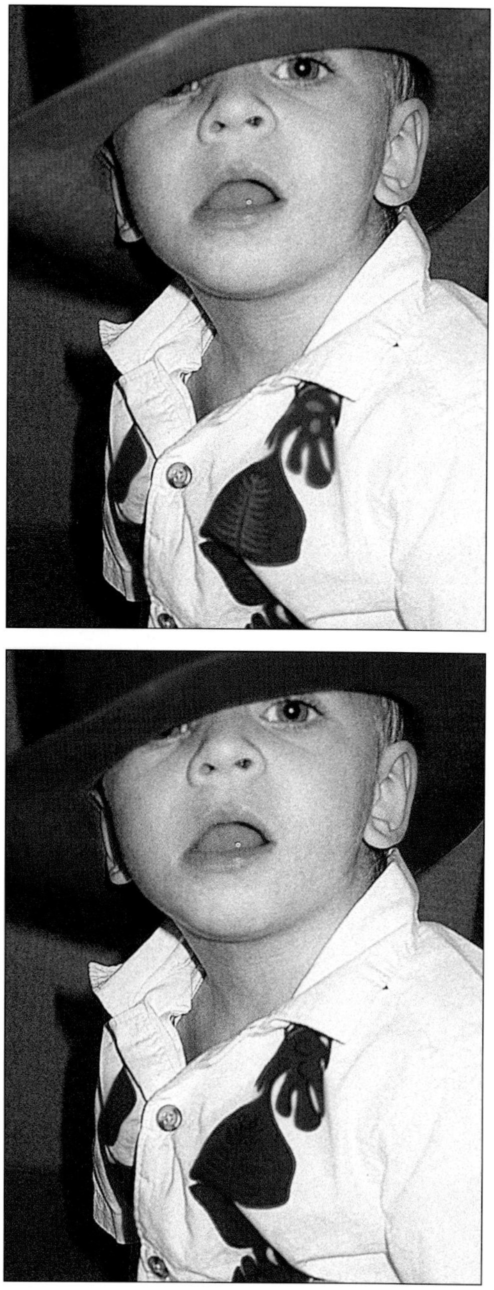

Careful painting in red and blue on a layer set to the color mode transformed the black & white image (top) into a much more interesting hand-colored one (bottom).

to activate it, and make sure that it is set to the Color mode.

Select the Brush tool and whatever size/hardness brush you like, and begin painting. Because you have set the layer mode to color, the color you apply with the brush will allow the detail of the underlying photo to show through.

If you're a little sloppy, use the Eraser tool (set to 100 percent in the Options bar) to remove the color from anywhere you didn't mean to put it. Using the Zoom tool to move in tight on these areas will help you work as precisely as possible.

If you want to add more than one color, you may wish to use more than one layer, all set to the Color mode.

When you've completed the "handcoloring," your image may be either completely or partially colored. With everything done, you can flatten the image and save it as you like.

Method 2

Here's a quick way to add a handcolored look in seconds—or, with a little refinement, to avoid having to select colors to handcolor with. This technique works only if you are starting with a color image.

The background layer was duplicated and the color removed. Then its opacity was set to 90 percent, allowing a little color to show through. The area over one rose was erased completely, allowing the underlying color image to show through.

FOR BETTER PAINTING

It can be tricky to paint on an image using your mouse. For better control, consider investing in a graphics tablet. Alternately, you can use selections to help you stay inside the lines with your painting.

Begin by duplicating the background layer (by dragging it onto the duplication icon at the bottom of the Layers palette).

Next, remove the color from the background copy by going to Enhance>Adjust Color>Remove Color. The image will turn black & white—but by reducing the opacity of the new layer you can allow the colors from the underlying photo to show through as much or as little as you like. Try setting the layer opacity to 80 percent for a subtly colored image.

To create the look of a more traditional black & white handcolored image, set the opacity of the desaturated layer to 100 percent and use the Eraser tool to reveal the underlying photo. Adjust the Eraser's opacity to allow as much color to show through as you like.

For a very soft look, set the opacity of the desaturated layer to about 90 percent (just enough to let colors show through faintly) and use the Eraser tool (set to about 50 percent) to erase areas where you want an accent of stronger color to appear.

RESTORING AN IMAGE

Very few images can be fixed with only one tool. In most cases, you'll need to employ several tools, combining their functions to make the needed corrections and enhancements.

The first step when restoring an image is to make a quick visual analysis and create a to-do list of things to fix. For this image, the list included the following points:

1. There were several spots and specks on the photo—as well as a few areas where the surface had torn away.
2. The photo was faded and yellowed. It had also lost some contrast.
3. The blue ink had also faded, making the inscription difficult to read.

Original image.

The first step was to correct the damaged areas and the spots and specks. Since these were small and scattered across the photograph, the Clone Stamp tool was used to sample nearby data and copy it over the damaged areas.

The next step in the restoration of this photograph was to remove the yellow color cast. This could have been accomplished using a number of different tools (Auto Color Correction,

Damaged area before correction.

Area after correction with the Clone tool.

The original image (left). The image after removing the yellow color cast with the Color Cast Correction command (center). The image after contrast correction with the Levels (right).

Color Variations, etc.). Since this is a black & white image, though, the easiest way to remove the color cast was to use Color Cast Correction (see page 46). The Levels were then used to adjust the contrast (see page 60–61).

The inscription had become a little faded. This was enhanced in two ways.

First, the Hue/Saturation command was used to increase saturation of the blue tones. This worked well since it was the only blue in the image.

To fill the gaps in the ink, the Brush tool was selected. Using the Eyedropper tool, the ink color was set as the foreground color. The brush size (after a couple of tries) was matched as closely as possible to the width of the ink line, and the hardness was set to about 70 percent to create relatively sharp edges.

Next, a new layer was created and activated in the Layers palette. After zooming in tight on the inscription (using the Zoom tool), the letters were traced with the Brush tool set to 50-percent opacity. Special attention was paid to areas where gaps occurred in the original writing.

When complete, the layer was set to the Multiply layer mode, making the painted areas on the layer blend in well with the original ink underneath, and darkening the combination slightly, for easier reading.

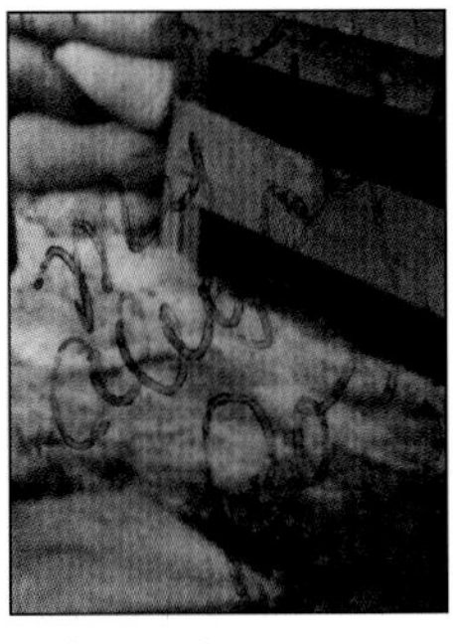

Before enhancement.

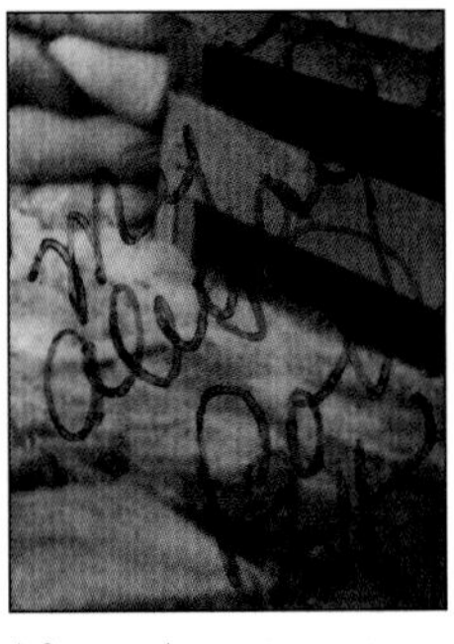

After enhancement.

Final image.

COMPOSITING IMAGES

Combining two images into one in a realistic way (called compositing) is extremely difficult with traditional photographic techniques—but Elements offers the controls you need to accomplish it seamlessly.

Originally, one of the most interesting uses for digital imaging was to combine elements of two images in a realistic way. While it's no longer a *primary* reason to use digital, compositing can still be a fun exercise.

The criteria for selecting images to composite should be rigorous. For realistic results, the direction and quality of lighting should be very similar in both. It helps, too, if all of the elements are well exposed and have no major color problems. Also, check to make sure the focus is correct. A softly focused subject in the midst of a sharply focused group will not look realistic.

Look at the images carefully and decide which one contains more of the material you want to retain in the final image. In this case, the theater (above right) will be the background. The only part of the other image that will be used is the figure in the center of the frame (above left). Therefore, the material to be imported into the background photograph (the woman) was selected using the Lasso and Magic Wand tools—adding to and subtracting from selections as needed.

The selection was then feathered to soften the edges and make them a little less obvious when moving the selected subject into the theater image. (Feathering the selection about 2 pixels is usually a good place to start.)

These images meet the lighting, exposure and focus criteria for compositing.

The selected area was then copied (Edit>Copy) and pasted (Edit>Paste) into a new layer in the theater image.

Once this was done, the rest of the job consisted of fine-tuning the components to make them blend as seamlessly as possible. Correct positioning of the new element on the new layer was the first task. To do this accurately, look at the scale of the imported material. Does it need to be changed in order to make sense with the subjects around it? Then, think about perspective. If your background image (as here) shows a scene in the distance, the subject must be at a correct size in relation to its apparent distance from the camera. In the images

Good placement.

Bad placement.

Shadow distorted to match other shadows in scene.

Top of shadow selected and distorted to run up the wall.

to the left, you can see the difference between reasonably good perspective and an obviously wrong one. In each image, the figure size remained the same; only the position changed.

Next, look at the color, brightness, and contrast of the new element in relation to the background. Correct any problems using the Levels or one of the other image-adjustment controls.

With the image almost complete, the only thing missing was the woman's shadow. Everything else in the image has long, dark shadows; adding one to the woman enforced the realism of the effect.

To add the shadow, the layer containing the subject was duplicated in the Layers palette. After activating the new layer, the Brightness/Contrast control (Enhance>Adjust Brightness/Contrast> Brightness/Contrast) was set to –100 on both sliders, making the subject go black on this layer.

Next, the Image>Transform>Distort command was used to drag the top of the new layer down diagonally. Since the shadow needed to bend up onto a wall, a second selection was made of the area of the shadow that would be on the wall. The Distort command was then used a second time to adjust this area.

With the basic outline of the shadow in place, the Gaussian Blur filter (set to 5 pixels) was used to create a softer edge on the shadow. The final step was to make the shadow more transparent by reducing the opacity of the layer it was on. In this case, the opacity was set to 30 percent.

Final composited image.

WEB AND PRINT GRAPHICS

Want to design digital scrapbook pages for your family album or create a must-see website? Here are some ideas for visually appealing effects that will add a professional polish to your project.

Using Elements isn't just about making your photos look better—it's also great for creating graphics. Whether or not these graphics include photos is up to you!

Plan for Output

Before you put a lot of work into creating a graphic, do take the time to make sure you are creating it at the right size and resolution. A little planning will save you a lot of frustration.

Design Basics

With Elements, you have complete control over the colors, size, and placement of the elements in your graphics. Take advantage of this and don't settle for just "okay." If you don't have much experience with graphic design, consider picking up a book for beginners (*The Non-Designer's Design Book* by Robin Williams [Peachpit Press, 1994] is a great one). You'll be surprised how a few simple changes to a design can make it suddenly spring to life.

Buttons and Banners

If you're creating a web site, why settle for simple text links when you can create a stylish button instead? Once you've created your button, consult your web-design software for how to put it in your page and define it as a link. Don't limit yourself to using effects like these on your web site, though—snazzy buttons and banners can work great in lots of other design project, too.

The buttons shown below were all created in Elements by opening a new document with a white background, then creating a new layer. On the layer, the desired shape of the button was selected (using one or more of the selection tools or the Custom Shape tool). It was then filled with a solid color or gradient, and layer effects were applied. As

There are limitless options for creating buttons in Elements. A few ideas are shown to the left—but you can also try making buttons out of photos, adding text to buttons, and much more!

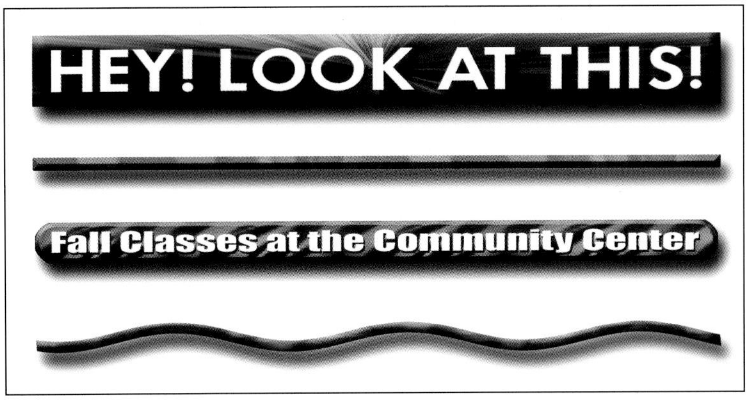

Banners and rules normally run horizontally to help divide sections in a design, but they can also be used vertically to set off important information from other text or images.

you can see, the results can be extremely varied.

Banners containing text and rules normally stretch across a page and help to divide sections of the page so viewers can navigate more easily. They can be created in exactly the same way as buttons—you just choose a different shape.

Background Photos

Very light, low contrast images (often in black & white or toned in another color) make great backgrounds for text or other images. The rule of thumb: make the image as light as you can stand it, then make it a little lighter. The image must be truly subtle—especially when you want to use text over it.

An easy way to achieve this effect is to open the Hue/Saturation dialog box (see pages 46–47). Click the Colorize box and adjust the Hue slider to render the image in a single color. Then, set the lightness very high (for the image below it was set to 80).

Background Patterns

Abstract images are another popular background choice. There are countless ways to make them in Elements. Running multiple filters (or the same one many times) can produce some very interesting looks. The Wave filter works particularly well for turning photos into unrecognizable patterns. You can also use the painting tools to create shapes and colors, then blur them or distort them in other ways that make them look more interesting. In fact, that's how the wavy blue pattern on the front of this book was created.

Very light, low-contrast images make great backgrounds for web pages and other designs. Here, a photo of a field of flowers was used as the background for a community garden's web site. The overlying photos have drop shadows applied to their layers, and blue buttons were used to highlight the links.

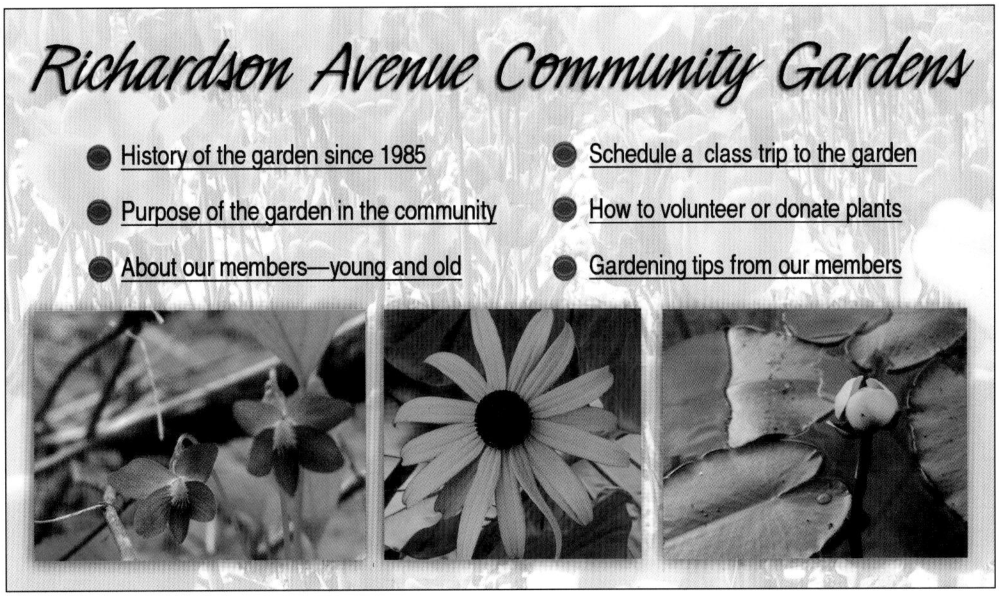

PANORAMIC IMAGES

Creative types have been combining photos since the beginning of photography—but doing it digitally certainly works a lot better than the old scissors-and-glue method!

Panoramic images are created digitally by shooting a sequence of images and then combining them into one photograph.

Shooting the Images

When you decide to make a panoramic image you'll need to plan to do so *before* you start shooting.

Whether you shoot film or digital, you'll want to select a mid-range lens (neither telephoto nor wide angle)—this would be about a 50mm lens on a 35mm camera. If you are using a point-and-shoot with a zoom lens, set it about halfway out. It might seem like a good idea to use a wide-angle lens for panoramics, but this will cause distortion at the edges of images, making them impossible to join together seamlessly.

When you start shooting, select one exposure setting and focus setting and

When you aren't careful about your lens setting, focus point, exposure, and the other details when shooting your original images, Elements won't be able to seamlessly merge your photographs into a unified whole. The results might initially look okay, but when you zoom in, as seen in the circular area to the left, the problems are evident. The architectural elements just don't match up properly and the exposure on the floor is way off.

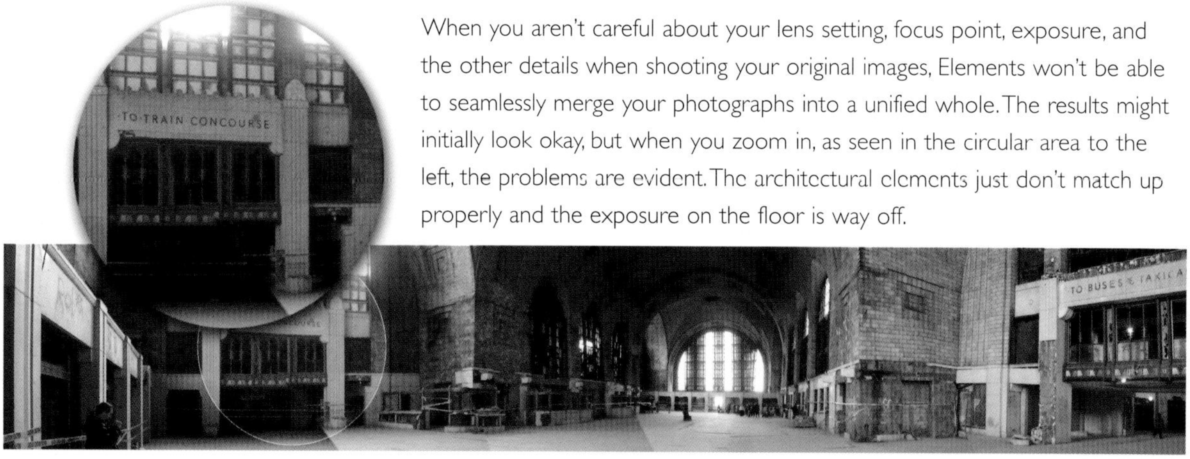

To create a seamless panoramic, try shooting from a tripod.

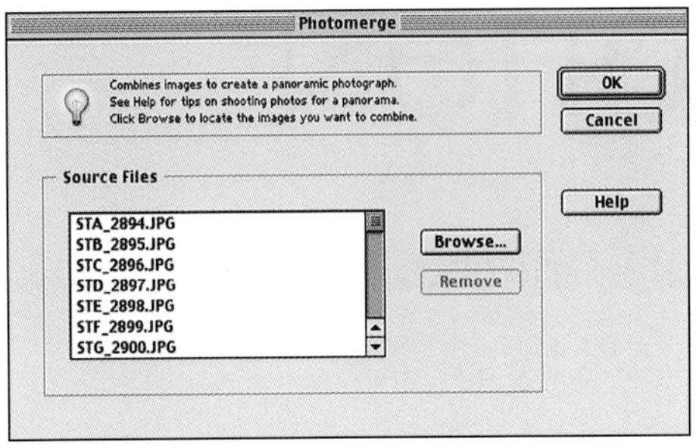

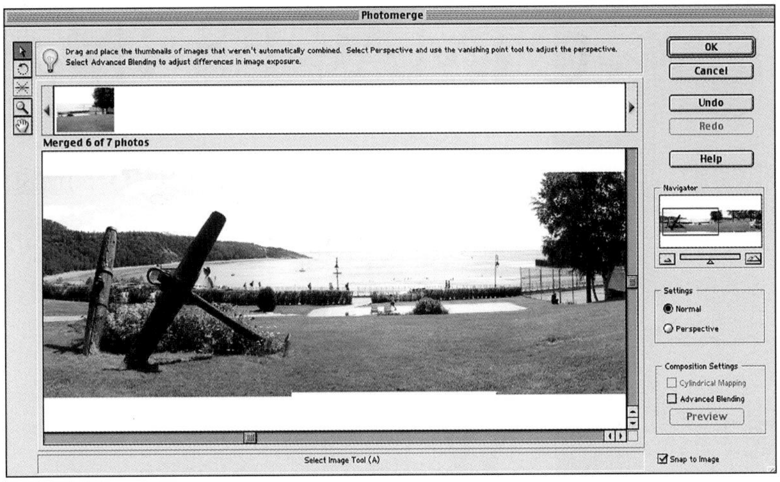

In the first Photomerge dialog box (above), click Browse to select the images you want to merge. In the second Photomerge box (right), make sure all the images are positioned correctly, then hit OK.

stick to it. The idea is to create the impression of a single image, and that won't happen if some sections are lighter/darker than others, or if the focus suddenly shifts from the foreground to the background.

It's also important to maintain a consistent camera height (for best results, use a tripod and rotate the camera as you take each shot).

Let's imagine you are standing facing the part of the scene that you want to have on the left edge of your final panoramic. Lift the camera and take the first shot, noting what is on the right-hand edge of the frame. Pivot slightly to the right and place the subject matter that was in the right-hand part of the first frame just inside the left edge of the second photo. Continue this process until you've taken enough images to cover the desired area. Ideally, you should have about a 10–20 percent overlap between the images.

If you're shooting digitally, check to see if your camera has a panoramic setting. If so, switching it to this setting will usually change the display on the LCD screen so that you can see the image you are about to shoot and the previous image side-by side, making it easy to set up each successive shot.

Photomerge

Once you've shot the images, combining them is a relatively simple procedure. When you go to File>Photomerge the first Photomerge window will open. Click Browse and select the images you want to merge. When all of the files appear in the Source Files window, hit OK and watch things start to happen.

When the second Photomerge window appears, Elements will try to place all of the photos in the correct position. If it can't, it will let you know. If this happens, the photos it can't place will appear as thumbnails at the top of the window. You can then drag them down into the main window and position them yourself. You can also click and drag the other images in the main window to reposition them if Elements doesn't do it correctly. When everything is in position, hit OK.

When the final image appears, it will usually have some uneven edges where the original photos overlap. Cropping the image will eliminate this and create the impression of a single image.

Making prints is still how most people tend to share their important photos, so make sure yours look great. For easy image sharing don't forget to consider online methods—you might even want to set up your own photography web site!

IMAGES IN ACTION

You've spent hours (or maybe just seconds) making the perfect image, so now what? It's time to share your creative genius with the world!

What's the point in creating a great image if you don't display it well? It is important to make sure your images look their best as you show them off, whether in prints on online.

Image Prep

Before outputting, flatten any layers you have created. Then, save the image in the required file format (usually JPEG or TIFF). Finally, double-check the size and resolution of your image.

Inkjet Printing

If you'll be printing your image on your inkjet printer, check the manual for the resolution it recommends. For the best results, take the time to read about the printer's software and the options it gives you for setting printing specifications. If it allows you to select the type of paper you will be printing on, be sure to select the one that best matches your paper—and do be sure to try printing on digital photo paper. It can be a little on the pricey side, but the results you'll get will far exceed what you can achieve on plain paper.

Lab Printing

Lab printing is really a win–win situation. The prints are real photographs (made on the same machine that used to print your images from negatives) so they look better and will last for years and years, unlike inkjet prints. Also, with even corner drugstores offering digital prints for about $.25, they actually cost less than printing at home. For online photo labs (like www.Snapfish.com and

CONTACT SHEETS

When you start working digitally, you'll probably take and make more images than you ever did with film—and why not, since they're basically free! This sheer volume of images can, however, make it something of a challenge to find a particular image when you want it. To make this easier, it's very useful to create contact sheets (File>Print Layouts>Contact Sheet). This lets you print lots of small images on one page and automatically puts the name of the file under each one. As you archive your work to CD-R or DVD-R, try to make a contact sheet for each disc and store it with the disc. When you do, you'll be able to find photos in a snap!

www.Shutterfly.com), you will normally save your files as JPEGs and upload the images directly to the website. To use a lab in your area, save your files as JPEGs on CD (or on a digital memory card) and just take them to the lab.

Picture Packages

The Picture Package function in Elements lets you print multiple copies of one image in an arrangement of sizes on one page. For home printing, this is especially efficient, since it allows you to make the most of each sheet you print. For lab printing, it may be more cost-effective to print smaller images individually. The exception can be with wallet-size prints, which sometimes command a premium price. Instead of paying this, you can create your own 8x10-inch page with sixteen wallet-size images and print it at the same price as any other 8x10-inch image.

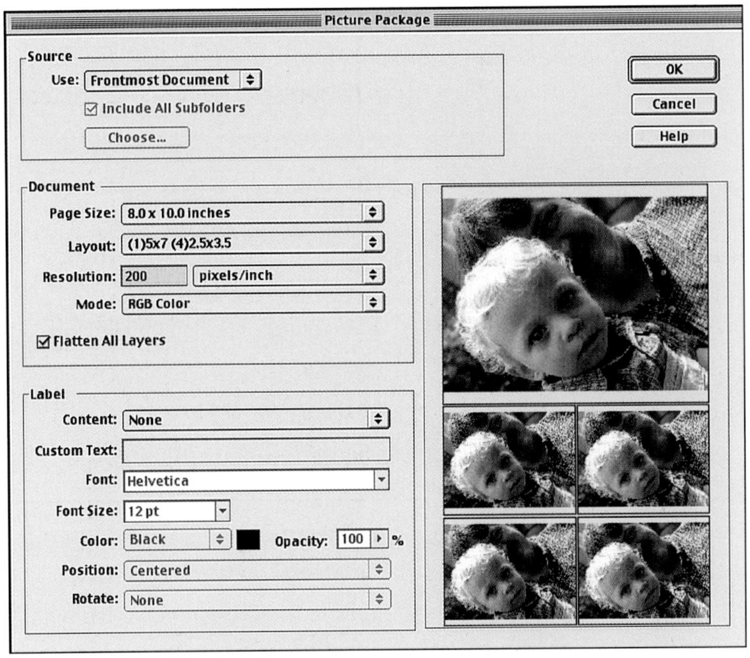

In the Picture Package dialog box, choose Foremost Document to work with a file you already have open, or set the Use menu to File and click Choose to select another image. Under Document, select the desired page size, layout, and resolution. You can label your photos using the controls at the bottom of the box.

Slide Shows

To create a slide show, go to File>Automation Tools>PDF Slideshow. From the dialog box, select the images for your slide show, how long each remains onscreen, and how to transition between them. Under Output File, click Choose to select a name for your slide show, then hit OK. To view the slide show, use Adobe Acrobat. This may already be on your computer, or you can download it for free at www.adobe.com.

Web Photo Gallery

Creating a Web Photo Gallery lets you automate the creation of a web page to display your photos. To start, move the photos you want on your page to one folder. Then, go to File>Create Web Photo Gallery and choose the gallery style from the pull-down menu (there are lots of looks to choose from). Enter your e-mail address if you want it to appear on the page, then (under Folders) select the folder of images for your page and a place to save the page.

The settings in the Options section at the bottom of the box vary with the style you choose. They let you add a banner (text that appears at the top of the gallery), control the fonts and colors used, adjust the size of the thumbnails and images in the gallery, and more.

When you've completed your web photo gallery, you can view it on your computer or upload it to your web site. Since all Internet service providers work a little differently, consult yours for specific information on how to do this.

Index

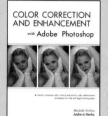

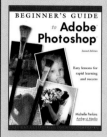

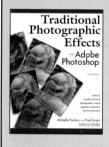

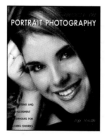